The Best 40 Days of My Life

A JOURNEY OF SPIRITUAL RENEWAL

THE BEST 40 DAYS OF MY LIFE

A JOURNEY OF SPIRITUAL RENEWAL

THROUGH

PRAYER, STUDY & MEDITATION

The Best 40 Days of My Life

THE BEST 40 DAYS OF MY LIFE

A JOURNEY OF SPIRITUAL RENEWAL

THROUGH

PRAYER, STUDY & MEDITATION

BY

MINISTER ONEDIA N. GAGE

THE BEST 40 DAYS OF MY LIFE

GOD'S WORDS

PSALM 1:1-2

¹ Blessed is the one
who does not walk in step with the wicked
or stand in the way that sinners take
or sit in the company of mockers,
² but whose delight is in the law of the Lord,
and who meditates on his law day and night.

PSALM 19:14

¹⁴ May these words of my mouth and this meditation of my heart
be pleasing in your sight,
Lord, my Rock and my Redeemer.

2 CORINTHIANS 4:16

¹⁶ Therefore we do not lose heart. Though outwardly we are wasting away, yet inwardly we are being renewed day by day.

ROMANS 12:2

² Do not conform to the pattern of this world, but be transformed by the renewing of your mind. Then you will be able to test and approve what God's will is—his good, pleasing and perfect will.

EXODUS 14:14

¹⁴ The Lord will fight for you; you need only to be still."

THE BEST 40 DAYS OF MY LIFE

Other Books by Onedia N. Gage

Are You Ready for 9th Grade . . . Again? A Family's Guide to Success
As We Grow Together Daily Devotional for Expectant Couples
As We Grow Together Prayer Journal for Expectant Couples
The Blue Print: Poetry for the Soul
From Two to One: The Notebook for the Christian Couple
Her Story: Bible Study
Her Story: Daily Devotional
Her Story: The Legacy of Her Fight
Her Story: The Legacy Journal
Her Story: Prayers and Journal
In Her Own Words: Notebook for the Christian Woman
In Purple Ink: Poetry for the Spirit
Living A Whole Life: Sermons Which Provide, Prompt, and Promote Life
Love Letters to God from a Teenage Girl
The Measure of a Woman: The Details of Her Soul
The Notebook: For Me, About Me, By Me
The Notebook for the Christian Teen
On This Journey Daily Devotional for Young People
On This Journey Prayer Journal for Young People
One Day More Than We Deserve Daily Devotional for the Growing Christian
One Day More Than We Deserve Prayer Journal for the Growing Christian
Promises, Promises: A Christian Novel
Tools for These Times: Timely Sermons for Uncertain Times
With An Anointed Voice: The Power of Prayer
Yielded and Submitted: A Woman's Journey for a Life Dedicated to God
Yielded and Submitted: A Woman's Journey for a Life Dedicated to God An Intimate Study
Yielded and Submitted: A Woman's Journey for a Life Dedicated to God Prayers and Journal

THE BEST 40 DAYS OF MY LIFE

LIBRARY OF CONGRESS

The Best 40 Days of My Life:

A Journey of Spiritual Renewal

Through

Prayer, Study and Meditation

All Rights Reserved © 2014

Onedia N. Gage

No part of this of book may be reproduced or transmitted in
Any form or by any means, graphic, electronic, or mechanical,
Including photocopying, recording, taping, or by any
Information storage or retrieval system, without the
Permission in writing from the publisher.

Purple Ink, Inc. Press

For Information address:
Purple Ink, Inc
P O Box 41232
Houston, TX 77241
www.purpleink.net
www.onediagage.com

ISBN:

978-1-939119-42-1

Printed in the United States

DEDICATION

HILLARY NICOLE

NEHEMIAH CHRISTIAN

WHAT I LEARN, SEE, EXPERIENCE AND ENDURE IS FOR YOU!

MAY GOD CONTINUE TO BLESS!

The Best 40 Days of My Life

A JOURNEY OF SPIRITUAL RENEWAL

DEAR FATHER GOD,

Lord, I love You! I know that it does not always look like I love You but I do, in my own sorry way.

Lord, when You gave me this devotional, I made up my own obstacles for me so that I could avoid addressing the issues I need to address in my own life and heart.

Lord, thank You for keeping me close to You. Even when and especially when I want to wander off or am led away. God, thank You for the guidance of the Holy Spirit and the example of Jesus Christ.

Lord, thank You for the gifts You have given me to share with You and others.

Father, thank You for caring for me and loving me and creating me and forgiving me. Your daughter needs you dearly!

Thank You God for blessing me with this devotional. I hope I have done what You have called me to do, that I have carefully detailed these words for the audience You have prepared for this message.

God, my Father, my Rock, and my Redeemer!

In Jesus' name, I pray this prayer!

Amen!

THE BEST 40 DAYS OF MY LIFE

A JOURNEY OF SPIRITUAL RENEWAL

DEAR FELLOW CHRISTIAN:

Greetings! We should seek God, panting after Him and His word. The word pant suggests that you have become thirsty. Worldly thirst is solved with water. Spiritual thirst is solved by God, and His word—drink His living word.

Immerse yourself in this to 40 day devotional! Your journey is certainly worth it. As you turn these pages, I am praying for you. Your spiritual renewal affects every aspect of your life! Your work, your children, your family, and your ministry are impacted by your spiritual journey.

Take time to spend time with our Master so that you can return to Him and enhance the rest of your life.

I am looking forward to your growth. Be honest with God and yourself. Be transparent with your testimony. I am looking forward to what God is doing for you and through you.

I picked the name based on the extravagance of the journey. These 40 days will be the best ones of your life!

Welcome to a fresh look at your life through the lens that God uses.

In God's service,

Onedia N. Gage

Onedia N. Gage

The Best 40 Days of My Life

A JOURNEY OF SPIRITUAL RENEWAL

THE SIGNIFICANCE OF 40

The number forty has been significant very early in our Christian journey.

40 years in the desert—original plan 11 days.

40 days of rain—Noah was assigned to the ark.

40 days between Ash Wednesday and Easter.

40 days of Jesus' fasting.

Despite our best intentions, we extend God's plans because we are simply disobedient. As it was with Moses and the children of Israel, what God designed for eleven days, took a total of 40 years. During these 40 years, several lessons were learned, such as patience with God, not to complain, and the most importantly, to follow God's directions—and follow them in real time.

God called Noah to have his family and the animals live in an ark that Noah would build. This experience would increase Noah's faith and sharpen his perspective of God. Noah then understood what it means for God to trust you.

In America, there are forty days between Ash Wednesday and Resurrection Sunday. This time is used to fast so that we are completely focused on God.

4 Then Jesus was led by the Spirit into the wilderness to be tempted by the devil.[2] After fasting forty days and forty nights, he was hungry. **Matthew 4:1-2**

The forty days that Jesus spent alone in the wilderness was communion with God. He fasted and prayed for 40 days. When He left the wilderness, He began to preach. This monumental moment Jesus spent with God is significant for the closeness we likewise want to experience with God.

The act of Jesus fasting for forty days—Jesus fasted for forty days and nights in preparation for His journey to death, burial and resurrection. These forty days share with us the level of sacrifice we need to make in order to please God, to grow closer to Him and to seek God in an authentic manner because He is God and God alone.

THE BEST 40 DAYS OF MY LIFE

These forty days should reflect your willingness to hear from God, seek God, walk away from that which separates you from God, and share God.

These forty days will be used by God to reconnect you to Him. Use these forty days to purge and cleanse, unite and commune, build and intensify a great relationship with God.

Bring all of your questions for God to the forty days, expecting to have answers when you are done.

Jesus left the wilderness proof positive that we always need to make time to get alone with God.

Expect power and profound revelation.

What will God use this time to do in your life?

What will happen after these 40 days?

Use this time to spend great time with God.

40 DAYS FOR GOD!

A Journey of Spiritual Renewal

COMMITMENT COVENANT

Please read this covenant aloud and then sign it below:

Lord, I will follow where You lead.

Lord, I willingly accept Your love.

Lord, I know that I am running from Your will.

Lord, I know that I am in need of Your guidance for these next steps to follow Your will.

Lord, I will pray each day so that I can disclose my heart to You for You to repair.

Lord, I submit to You my total self through this study.

Lord, I will stop rejecting You through my storms.

Lord, I will not be ashamed of Your work in my life.

Lord, I promise to share the outcome of this study.

Lord, I will give You 100% of me so that You can get the best results possible which You planned for me in advance.

Lord, I know You love me and while I do not always accept that love as truth, I will do better about exhibiting the love You have for me.

Because I can be evident that the Lord is real!

Name: _____

Date: _____

THE BEST 40 DAYS OF MY LIFE

INSTRUCTIONS FOR USE

1. Pray.

2. Pray for your spiritual advancement.

3. Pray for your sensitivity to God's voice, the presence of the Holy Spirit, and the ability to obey according to what you hear.

4. Listen for God.

5. Answer the questions authentically.

6. Be ready to change for God's will to be done.

7. Pray.

8. Fast.

9. Share the work God is doing in your life.

10. Stay focused for the 40 days. Stay the course. God is waiting for you to do the work.

TABLE OF CONTENTS

God	25	War	105
Jesus Christ	29	Anger	109
Holy Spirit	33	Servant/Service	113
Love—The Definition	37	Ministry	117
Prayer	41	The Cup	121
Fasting	45	Fruit of the Spirit	125
Faith	49	The Armor	129
Praise	53	Image	133
Worship	57	His Protection	137
Meditation	61	His Provision	141
Study	65	His Power	145
Teach	69	Holiness	149
Disciple	73	Forgiveness	153
Gifts	77	Discipline	157
God's Voice	81	Compassion	161
Love—The Demonstration	85	Victory	165
A Walk	89	Revive	169
Healing	93	Heart	173
Still	97	Wisdom	177
Enemy	101	Renewal	181

A Journey of Spiritual Renewal

THE BEST

*40*DAYS

OF MY LIFE

The Best 40 Days of My Life

DAY ONE

GOD

GENESIS 1-GENESIS 2

God and God alone! For creating the Heavens and the Earth, God thank You. You desire a relationship with me. A relationship with me is important to You so it needs to be important to me. As I work daily on a relationship with You, please offer me Your guidance and leadership to help me make the mark of loving You.

I know that I have an obedience issue and an inability to be still and the propensity to help do Your work but my way, outside of Your will.

I thank You for forgiving me for my sins. Lord, I ask You to penetrate my heart God so that You can show me where I can grow. Upon that growth, please reveal where I can serve You and how I will help others.

Through Your sovereignty, I am spared and protected. I thank You for that protection so that I will know that it is in You Oh Lord, I put my trust. I do not know what You protect me from, I just say thank You.

Because of Your mercy, I know that You are able and willing to grant me the requests and desires of my heart. Thank You for the plans You have for me. As others meet me, may they see You Lord, and not my spoiled and rotten self. Lord, Please do not let my selfishness ruin what others need to see in order to unite or reunite them with You.

Lord, keep reminding me that I belong to You and that I am resolve to belong to You.

Lord, thank You for allowing me to show up for You when I teach, preach, serve and pray.

Lord, You loved me first. I am working to love You better—with my whole heart.

The Best 40 Days of My Life

DEAR GOD,

Lord God! Oh Lord, Our Lord, How excellent is Your name is all the Earth!

Lord afresh I thank You for Your grace and Your mercy. Lord, I know that Your love for me is extravagant. I thank You for loving me because You created me. I know that You love me despite of my ugly ways. I know that You love me even when I do not love myself.

Lord, thank You for forgiving me for my sins. You forgive me when I do not forgive myself or others.

Lord, thank You for healing me from physical illnesses. Lord, thank You for healing me from my broken heart. Lord, God, thank You for caring for me, providing a comforter for me.

Lord, the gifts and talents You have given me course through my veins. I am talented according to Your will. I pray I use those talents to enhance Your kingdom.

Lord, I will ever need You. I love You but You do not always see it because of my poor behavior—my sins.

Lord, thank You for providing for me, blessing me and protecting me. I know You have a high hedge of protection around me and I appreciate Your protection.

In Jesus' name, I pray these blessings.

Amen!

A JOURNEY OF SPIRITUAL RENEWAL

JOURNAL QUESTIONS:

1. HOW CAN I RELATE TO GOD BETTER?
2. HOW CAN I GROW CLOSER TO GOD?
3. HOW CAN I HEAR FROM GOD?
4. HOW CAN I MEET THE EXPECTATIONS OF GOD?
5. HOW DOES GOD WANT ME TO RESPOND TO HIM?

_____
_____
_____
_____
_____
_____
_____
_____
_____
_____
_____
_____

THE BEST 40 DAYS OF MY LIFE

DAY TWO

JESUS CHRIST

MATTHEW 1; JOHN 1:1-2

Jesus was born to die for our sins. Christ bore the weight of our sins and our burdens He bears. This is truly a task. When I consider how many sins that He died for, I shudder and stammer.

When people ask me who Jesus is, I become reverent immediately. I may be solemn. I may be silent. I am joyful. I am expectant. I am reverent. Jesus took the risk and paid the cost for my sins and did not leave one out.

My favorite details about Jesus are that He is a teacher, prayer warrior, and the definition of love. Jesus spent a lot of time teaching—outside, hillside, and bankside. Jesus is a teacher of all things. He teaches in parables and offers wisdom and these lessons and instructions are sometimes subtle, yet applicable life-long. He teaches through His examples of His life. His walk and His practices MATCH!

Jesus even teaches us to pray. Jesus is our prayer warrior and our example of prayer. When the scripture shares Jesus' prayer life, the scripture shared that He is often praying and alone. Jesus takes our needs and burdens to His Father and Our God, and seeks a solution for our concerns. Jesus' prayers to His Father are comprehensive and transparent. Jesus is submissive in prayer. Jesus is encouraging in prayer and encourages us through prayer. Jesus encourages us to pray. Jesus then sent us another intercessor of the Holy Spirit. The Holy Spirit is our gift—comforter, which is who prays only the will of God with groans that we may not understand. Jesus is our definition of LOVE. No other definition exists! He was born to DIE for my sins!

The Best 40 Days of My Life

DEAR GOD,

Thank You for Jesus Christ! Lord, Your sacrifice is my ultimate gift! When I teach about You, I admit that if I had to sacrifice my child, I may have disappointed You. Lord God, thank You for Christ. Thank You for His prayer, His love, His leadership, and His discipleship.

Dear God, thank You for the miracles He performed causing me to understand the ability You have in my life—up close and from a distance.

Dear God, I am thankful for His intercession on my behalf. Jesus, thank You for loving me, helping me to be obedient, offering me the example to follow which allows me to follow Your will.

Dear God, thank You for keeping Your promises to me so that my life would be made whole.

Thank You God for Jesus as my light in a world that honors darkness. Jesus offers me strength and equips me to handle my friends and enemies. In every season, Jesus is there and as an example for my life, He has experienced everything that I have and more than I would endure.

As I consider my relationship with Christ, I realize that I am in need of more time in prayer and meditation.

Lord, I love You! I need You! Thank You for my Savior! Thank You for the privilege of using His name to ask for my desires!

In Jesus' name I pray!

Amen.

JOURNAL QUESTIONS:

1. WHY DOES JESUS LOVE ME?
2. HOW DO I KNOW HE LOVES ME?
3. HOW DOES HE KNOW THAT I LOVE HIM?
4. WHAT KIND OF RELATIONSHIP DOES JESUS WANT WITH ME?
5. WHAT KIND OF RELATIONSHIP DO I WANT WITH JESUS?
6. WHAT DOES HIS SACRIFICE MEAN TO ME?

The Best 40 Days of My Life

DAY THREE

HOLY SPIRIT

JOHN 16:5-16

As Jesus uses this opportunity to share the Holy Spirit, Jesus introduces the Holy Spirit to encourage me. This encouragement is alive today.

In order to benefit from a fulfilling relationship with the Holy Spirit, I have to trust and not question. As I close the gap between me and the Holy Spirit, I am required to submit to the Holy Spirit my needs, my prayers, my desires, my health, my mind, my heart, and my soul.

The Holy Spirit is on assignment to keep me within God's will. I do not envy the Holy Spirit because the Holy Spirit has to corral my racing mind and outlandish heart.

My goal is to become closer to the Holy Spirit as well as be able to recognize the will of God.

Submit to the Holy Spirit because of God.

Surrender to the will of God because of the Holy Spirit.

Submit to the Holy Spirit because He is on my side.

The Best 40 Days of My Life

DEAR GOD,

Father, You sent a Spirit to me as a gift through Jesus Christ!

Thank You for designing the Holy Spirit to intercede on my behalf, listening to me, understanding Your will for my life, and speaks to me to guide me and confirm what I need to act upon.

Lord, thank You for the Holy Spirit to translate my prayers into prayers which communicate Your will to Your own ears for hearing and actions.

Thank You for the power of the Holy Spirit. Thank You for allowing the Holy Spirit to exercise in my life Your will and Your desires for me. Thank You for the guidance of the Holy Spirit. I thank You for the guidance through the urging of the Holy Spirit in my heart, soul and mind. Thank You for keeping me in Your keeping power, under Your sovereignty, under the protection of Your hand, under the grace of Your heart, and under the mystery of Your love.

The Holy Spirit, I thank You for Your help for my soul. As I have to change and make choices based on what I think I know, I know that God is watching me and the Holy Spirit is assigned to me so that I am never away from You God.

In Jesus' name I pray.

Amen.

JOURNAL QUESTIONS:

1. WHO IS THE HOLY SPIRIT?
2. HOW DOES THE HOLY SPIRIT HELP ME?
3. DO I KNOW HOW THE HOLY SPIRIT SOUNDS AND FEELS?
4. HOW CAN I BE CLOSER TO THE HOLY SPIRIT?
5. HOW DOES THE HOLY SPIRIT KNOW WHAT TO DO?

_____
_____
_____
_____
_____
_____
_____
_____
_____
_____
_____
_____
_____

The Best 40 Days of My Life

DAY FOUR

LOVE: THE DEFINITION

JOHN 3:16; 1 CORINTHIANS 2:9; EPHESIANS 5:25-27

God, why do I question You? You have defined love for me. You told me about love. You told me how to love. You showed me love, in an ultimate manner—You sacrificed Your Son.

You defined love as infinite—how long and high and wide and deep. You have exhibited Your love to me. Because of that love, I am secure. I know that I don't act secure or appear secure but I am supposed to be. As I examined the meaning of love and the actions that results from love by how I should love forward.

When we are able to love, initiate love and respond to love in a loving manner, then we actually understand love and are truly immersed in love. As we understand how to demonstrate the definition of love, we then can love others and help them to be loving. As we discuss love, we need to remember that all people do not feel love. As those who demonstrate the definition, we can create love within others. Where love exists, there is a freedom. This freedom allows for relief and the ability to relax and to achieve all the other things you desire.

Love is fuel! God has shaped me with fuel to achieve His will. Share the fuel with others. Use that fuel to forgive myself later.

LOVE with intention.

THE BEST 40 DAYS OF MY LIFE

DEAR GOD,

Love extravagantly! Lord, when You sent Your Only Son to die for my sins, You did the ultimate! Your love is unmatched and unsurpassed! Lord, I pale in comparison to what You exhibit toward us. I do love You!

I know that You deserve more from me! I know I should be able to love You more and more authentically. I don't need another reason to love—You have always given me so many. Lord, as I grow closer to You, I know that love is important! You deserve my love. You created me to love.

Lord, I ask that You help me to soften my heart so that love comes easier. Lord, I ask You to help me realize that everyone is not going to love me the way I think they ought. I pray Your gift of love through others so that I can also love others the way You command.

Thank You for love that fills and heals.

Lord, Your love is dynamic and complicated. I could not possibly duplicate.

Lord, help me to receive Your love better, as well as love others as You command.

I love You. Please forgive me for not doing better.

In the powerful name of Jesus, I pray and ask these blessings.

Amen.

JOURNAL QUESTIONS:

1. HOW DO I DEFINE LOVE?
2. WHO DO I LOVE?
3. WHO DO I ALLOW TO LOVE ME?
4. WHY DO I HAVE A HARD TIME LOVING OTHERS?
5. WHAT DOES GOD'S LOVE MEAN TO ME?
6. HOW DO I SHARE LOVE WITH OTHERS?

The Best 40 Days of My Life

DAY FIVE

PRAYER

2 CHRONICLES 7:14

There are a few points which God makes directly—one of which is prayer. God commands that we pray. God states that if I would pray to Him with an humbleness and with attention to His commands, He would heal my land.

God deserves our prayers. He designs us to pray to Him for our needs, His praise, our forgiveness, His directions and our communion. Prayer is a place of communion for our relationship to grow and to flourish.

The steps God describes in this verse are to be applied to our current lives. The main element is humility in our spirits. We approach with humility and without entitlement and without pride.

Prayer then needs to be direct and authentic. God has commanded us to turn away from out wicked, sinful ways. God wants us to give Him our best efforts to live righteously. God wants us to live like He is God. We sometimes get off track and create idols of other things which interfere with the relationship we have with God.

Our prayer life will reveal where those idols have developed. Further, our prayer life is the only way to have the healing we desperately need. Our 'land' needs to be considered as our hearts, our minds, our souls, and our bodies. We are in desperate need of healing. This healing will allow us to love, grow, forgive and give of ourselves to others the way God designed.

Prayer is not a time to complain. It is time to share with God your perception of His needs, while fully intending to complete His work.

When He heals our essential elements, then He can get the best out of us. He needs the best of us.

THE BEST 40 DAYS OF MY LIFE

DEAR FATHER GOD,

Thank You for the ability to pray. Thank You for the power of prayer. Thank You for the presence of the Holy Spirit as I pray. Thank You for the intercession of the Holy Spirit when I pray and especially when I do not.

Thank You for Jesus who teaches us how to pray, demonstrates a healthy prayer life, and teaches us that prayer is the practice of a disciplined disciple.

Lord, thank You for hearing me when I pray. I know that I doubt often, thank You for answering me anyway. I know that I am impatient. Thank You for Your impeccable timing in my life.

Lord, thank You for listening to me when I whine about my 'light afflictions' as if You are not real and that my situation is hopeless.

Lord, thank You for answering me, being patient with me, loving me enough to forgive me and allowing me to intercede on behalf of others.

Thank You for hearing me, Lord!

In Jesus' name.

Amen.

JOURNAL QUESTIONS:

1. WHAT DO I NEED TO SAY TO GOD?
2. HOW DO I KNOW GOD HEARS ME?
3. WHAT DOES GOD EXPECT OF ME DURING PRAYER?
4. WHAT DOES PRAYER MEAN TO GOD?
5. WHY WILL PRAYER AFFECT MY SPIRITUAL LIFE?
6. WHY DO I HAVE TROUBLE PRAYING? FINDING TIME? FINDING WHAT TO SAY?

_____
_____
_____
_____
_____
_____
_____
_____
_____
_____
_____
_____

The Best 40 Days of My Life

DAY SIX

FASTING

2 SAMUEL 12:21—23; MATTHEW 6:16—18

Fasting is an act of obedience to God designed to demonstrate to God that you can be willingly purged from those elements which complicate our relationship with God.

David fasts in order to repent. He considers that God may change His mind because he has humbly repented and fasted to show his sincerity. God does forgive David but does not change the consequence.

Fasting is the sincerest form of sacrifice. When you are fasting, your behavior should reflect humility and remorse. What we do not do is expect that God is going to do what we want Him to do differently than what He decided. When we do not present ourselves to God with the attitude of if I fast then God will change His mind, we exercise humility and love. If we are fasting authentically with a genuine remorse and a sincere heart, then we will be received well by God.

Jesus says that we should not look pitiful as we fast. Likewise, do not share that you are fasting. Prayer is important for fasting. Prayer and fasting are companions. Fasting is not limited to food. Fasting is eliminating elements that interrupt your relationship with God. This means that you should consider fasting from social media, cell phone usage, television, and shopping or whatever else that entangles you.

Fasting is a retreat for you and God so that you can be restored. While David still lost that son, he and Bathsheba were blessed with Solomon, the next king.

Fasting is critical for the best relationship with God.

The Best 40 Days of My Life

DEAR GOD,

Lord, help me to fast so that I can grow closer to You! Lord, help me have wisdom to know when to fast and what to remove from my life. I know that I need more discipline. Lord, I beg Your hand of guidance around me so that I fast in the right season and for the right reasons.

Lord, I pray that as I fast, I do so to glorify You and not for my own edification. I love You and will fast as You will for me to do so.

Lord, I need You and Your guidance and Your leadership. I learned that You remove those elements in my life which separate me from You.

Lord, remind me of The Vine and me as the branch. As the branch, I can be pruned. These fasting periods prune me so that I am closer to the Christian that You created.

Lord, I offer You parts of myself that no other person can see and nor access.

Lord, I seek to honor You will all that I am and all that I am to be. To God be the glory which You so richly deserve.

In Your Awesome Son Jesus' name!

Amen.

JOURNAL QUESTIONS:

1. WHY DO I FAST?
2. WHY SHOULD I FAST?
3. IS FASTING LED BY GOD?
4. WHEN SHOULD I FAST?
5. WHAT IS THE PURPOSE OF FASTING?

THE BEST 40 DAYS OF MY LIFE

DAY SEVEN

FAITH

HEBREWS 11:6; MATTHEW 14:31

Faith is a mystery to some people, however faith is not unclear, while we treat it that way. I am faithful. I have faith. You do too. How do you know that? You are reading this page. You got out of bed this morning after God woke you up.

Faith is believing that an outcome will take place regardless of what the circumstances appear to be. Faith is a companion to work. Believe and do. There is a faith when you walk with one foot in front of the other. There are areas where we take faith for granted but there are other areas when our faith is really challenged, so much so that we start to question our Christianity and our total belief in God.

Believe. What causes you to doubt when you should believe? Faith is believing in spite of all that you see and what you do not see. The other component of faith is work while you are waiting on the outcomes.

What does work look like? Work starts with getting out of bed. Work means finishing school. Work means sending your resume. Work means asking for what you are seeking. We cannot stop working but still want to do something.

Jesus visited a lame man by the pool. Jesus asked, "Do you want to walk?" The man replied with excuses, many excuses. Jesus asked him again. The man finally replied yes. Then he was able to walk (John 5:1-10). How many excuses do you use to stop your progress?

These excuses are stopping your faith from being active. It took faith to believe what Jesus said and then do the work.

Jesus said, "Take up your mat and walk."

Your faith requires you to take up your 'mat' and 'walk.'

THE BEST 40 DAYS OF MY LIFE

DEAR FATHER OF FAITH,

Based on faith of a Jesus Christ You created, sent and saved, I am called to a life of faith.

Lord, I beg Your forgiveness when I am less than faithful and mostly doubtful. I thank You for the calming influence over my life and through my heart.

Lord, as I walk through this life, I aim to please You! Lord, I want to please You through Your definition of faith for me. I need help being more faithful when storms are heavy and the way looks bleak.

Lord, help me to realize that I need to focus on You so that I do not lose faith and heart.

Lord, keep me whole, healthy, and wise, as I follow You at all times. When I question, and disrespectfully so, when my mind wanders with disdain about my current situation, when I forget that I am not in charge of my destiny nor my fate, God gently remind and restore me unto You.

Lord, You are worthy to hold faithful and be respected with the faith You required.

Not my will but Thine will be done!

In Your darling Son Jesus' name!

Amen.

JOURNAL QUESTIONS:

1. HOW DOES GOD WANT ME TO EXERCISE MY FAITH?
2. HOW DO I KNOW THAT I HAVE FAITH?
3. DO OTHERS NEED TO KNOW THAT I AM FAITHFUL?
4. WHAT DO I THINK ABOUT MY FAITH?

THE BEST 40 DAYS OF MY LIFE

DAY EIGHT

PRAISE

PSALM 139:14, 17

God deserves our praise! We were created to praise and worship God. If we do not praise and do not intend to praise, then why are we here?

We praise God because He created us. Consider how excited we are when a baby is born. We should praise Him with that very some excitement.

Do we know what praise is? As defined by God? Praise is defined as adoration for God, sharing who He is, what He does, how awesome He is, and who we are because of Him. Praise is the accolades we give God because He is God and God alone. Praise is already earned by God.

Unlike when we are praising each other or our children, God has already done everything He needs to ever do to earn our praise. God keeps your breathing, walking, talking, thinking, loving, sharing, and feeling. God does all of that even when we do not deserve to continue to do any of that. We were created praise Him. Consider what God gifted each with something which should prompt us to please Him. Without an excuse. Without prompting. We should crave the opportunity to praise Him.

Praise frees you spirit. When you authentically praise God, you have to release those issues which has you stuck at the bottom of that ocean. Those issues prohibit you from praising God. You are chained to your issues and those issues are stifling your authentic praise to God.

Praise God. Start to praise God. Praise Him in an authentic way so that He can free you from your issues. You may cry. There will be a time when you welcome those tears because you are now crying because you can feel God because you can praise Him again, or maybe it was the first time.

I like to praise God when I am in my car, when I am alone, so that I can praise Him loudly, unapologetically. I praise Him because He deserves it. God keeps His words and follows His plans, which include me.

The Best 40 Days of My Life

DEAR GOD,

As I consider my relationship with You, I am embarrassed for the amount of praise that I have neglected to give You. Lord, forgive me for not praising You enough. Lord, I praise You selfishly. I praise You sometimes because I want something or because I need something. Lord, help me to praise You because You are God—not for any other reason.

Lord, I wish to praise You in an authentic manner, where my heart is more pure—as close to Your original design of me as possible. Lord, I pray Your guidance as I learn to praise You authentically with a dedicated and committed spirit.

Lord, I owe You praise for the smallest and largest blessings alike. I want to grow so that I crave the place and time to praise You.

Lord, thank You for allowing me a second chance to praise You as I should, as I ought, like I should want to, and because You are my God, my Rock, and my Redeemer and my Savior.

Lord, I praise You as I pray that prayer in Jesus' name.

Amen.

JOURNAL QUESTIONS:

1. WHAT DOES MY PRAISE SAY TO GOD?
2. IS MY PRAISE WORTHY OF GOD?
3. DOES GOD VALUE MY PRAISE?
4. WHAT DOES MY PRAISE LOOK LIKE?

The Best 40 Days of My Life

DAY NINE

WORSHIP

PSALM 95:6-7; PSALM 100; 1 CORINTHIANS 14:26-40

Worship is designed to seek God in a reverent manner. Worship is outward adoration in a outwardly demonstrative manner. Worship is singing, saying hallelujah, and other outward expressions of adoration for God.

Worship can be scary because you then may not be in full control of yourself—as you worship, the Holy Spirit is in control. For those persons who worry about the thoughts of others, worship is hard for you.

When I was eight years old, a lady at church shouted and 'got happy.' She shouted and danced before the Lord. Her hair was messed up. She was perspiring. She was crying. When she was done, she sat down. Some church members fanned her. Someone helped her out of her choir robe to help her cool off.

After church, I spoke with her. I asked her what happened. She said, "I got happy." At eight years old, she left me with a lot to ponder.

I asked myself did I love God enough because I did not get happy in that manner. I later asked myself if her worship and mine needed to be the same. The answer is no, our worship will not be the same all of the time.

Further, we worship based on what our needs are at the time. Similar to praise, authentic worship frees you from your bondage. This bondage is self-inflicted and self-perpetuated.

She was uninhibited in her worship but it did not mean that we loved God any less than the other. She showed me not be afraid to worship in front of God when there is an audience.

God is our Creator and who we can be proud of, and He will honor my authentic worship. Worship is a thank you and an appreciation for God's sovereignty, mercy and grace, God's love and forgiveness. Worship God because God is. Worship is key to your spiritual oneness with God and your personal freedom!

The Best 40 Days of My Life

DEAR LORD,

While I do not need any reasons to worship You, I have many! I have many reasons to worship You, Lord God! In a manner that would authenticate that I belong to You! God, there are times when I miss the mark of worship!

God, there are times when I should worship you but I choose otherwise. God, there are times when I should seek to worship You but I get distracted!

Father for those seasons in my life when I have completely neglected Your worship, I beg Your forgiveness. I am a sorry vessel, Lord, to not voluntarily worship You.

Lord, help me to worship You in spirit! Lord, help me to worship You in truth! Lord, I know that all of my behavior does not exhibit how much I love and adore You but I do! I need Your help!

Lord, I love You and beg to worship through the distractions, especially through the storms and always when You call me to worship You. You called Moses and Hannah, Noah and David, John the Baptist and Mary, and Jesus to worship You. Lord, I want to hear You more when You speak and obey Your voice.

With an open heart to worship In Jesus' name.

Amen.

A JOURNEY OF SPIRITUAL RENEWAL

JOURNAL QUESTIONS:

1. WHAT IS THE DIFFERENCE BETWEEN WORSHIP AND PRAISE?
2. HOW DO I WORSHIP GOD?
3. IS GOD PLEASED WITH MY WORSHIP?
4. WHAT DO OTHERS THINK OF MY WORSHIP?
5. IS MY WORSHIP AUTHENTIC?
6. HOW DO I KNOW MY WORSHIP IS AUTHENTIC?

THE BEST 40 DAYS OF MY LIFE

DAY TEN

MEDITATION

PSALM 1:2; PSALM 19:14

Meditation is the ability to study then consider what you have studied. During this meditation time, you will likely hear from God.

Meditation requires two elements: (1) time, and, (2) your ability to be still. Meditation is most effective when you are still and take the time to do it. Further, meditation happens when you can clear your mind and focus totally on God.

For many of us, this is extremely difficult. We do not give God unlimited time to do His work. We do not clear our mind to study God and His words. Lastly, we cannot be still! Meditation is next to impossible.

Effective meditation yields a closeness to God. God is listening and waiting. Meditation cements our knowledge and understanding of God and His word.

Meditation is worth the time and the stillness. Absorb the word of God in a mental and emotional space where God is priority. Meditation keeps us grounded because we have to surrender our complete focus on God. Meditation is not an event for multi-tasking.

Surrender to God's leadership. Start in your favorite scripture book and chapter. Read it. Maybe two or three times. Pray, asking God what did He want you to understand, do, share, and know. Realize that we are vessels where what we learn and know is not for us to harbor and keep to ourselves. It is for the use of those who you come into contact with.

Meditation should help you grow. Help you grow up. Help you grow into your complete calling.

How close do you want to be to God? Meditation closes that gap!

The Best 40 Days of My Life

OH HOLY GOD,

May the words of my mouth and the meditations of my heart be pleasing in Thine sight, my Rock and my Redeemer! Lord, I need to be more attentive to You through my meditations and the content of my heart.

Lord, heal my heart form the brokenness that it has experienced, and close the gap between my heart and Yours. So I can be proud to present my whole heart to You.

Lord, grow me up so that I can be silent and not be afraid. Lord, mature me so that I can sit still and posture myself so that I can hear from You! Lord, help me to still my mind so that my mind can meditate purely on You! Lord, help me to clear the mechanism so that I can hear You and respond to You in real time!

Be still and know that I am God. Help me to embrace Your words so that I can commune with You, hear from You, be obedient to You and serve You.

Lord, share Your secrets with me about Your will for my life. Lord, please allow me to be sensitive to the Holy Spirit so that I can surrender to Your calling of meditation.

Thank You for the example of meditation through Jesus Christ!

Amen!

JOURNAL QUESTIONS:

1. WHAT DOES MEDITATING MEAN?
2. WHAT DOES MEDITATING MEAN TO GOD AND HIS WORD?
3. WHAT DOES MEDITATING DO FOR MY SPIRITUAL LIFE?
4. WHEN DO I MEDITATE?
5. WHY AM I ANXIOUS ABOUT MEDITATING?
6. WHY DO I MEDITATE?

THE BEST 40 DAYS OF MY LIFE

DAY ELEVEN

STUDY

2 TIMOTHY 7:15

In all of our life's endeavors, study is required. Study is to immerse yourself in your material. I know people who can regurgitate statistics like they were speaking their names. Do we know God like that?

What was the last scripture you learned? Can you share it with others? What do you know about God? Can you teach someone else about God?

How much time do you spend studying the work of Your Creator?

How much time do you spend studying the nature of Your Creator?

How much time do you work on the knowledge of God?

How much of what you know do you use to make great decisions according to what God has designed?

How much of what you know can you apply for the growth of others?

How much of what you know do you use to grow closer to God?

Do you remember the study skills from school? Do you remember how to study?

Do you write each scripture until you know it?

Do you say it aloud until you know it? When do you internalize the message the scripture presents?

God knows us very well—better than we know ourselves. It seems like we would crave the time we are able to spend with God. Our study will enhance, enliven and enlighten who we are. There is good news in the Bible. With so much happening in the world, we need some good news. The good news will keep us on course. His word will keep us engaged.

Study is an investment. It shows God that we are serious about our relationship with Him. We need to examine ourselves to understand why we do not want to spend time with the Supplier of all the we have.

THE BEST 40 DAYS OF MY LIFE

DEAR FATHER GOD,

I crave the time to spend with You, Lord. God, I need more time with You! I don't seem to have enough time to spend time with You. Lord, I want to You to know that You did not create me in vain. I crave You, Lord and studying Your word is an indication that I love You because I spend time with You.

Lord, I want to know more about You through the study of You through Your word. Lord, I need to know more about You. Lord, if I love You like I say that I do then I should study. My study demonstrates of getting to know You and that I have a genuine interest in our relationship.

Lord, I profess that I am saved because of You. Because I want to know more about He that saved me, I study.

Lord, thank You for allowing me to study to show myself approved as the Christian You have called.

I am anxious to go deeper in Your word. I desire to exhibit knowledge that demonstrates Your calling on my life.

Lord, help me prioritize my time so that I have time for study.

In Jesus' name!

Amen!

JOURNAL QUESTIONS:

1. WHY DO I STUDY?
2. WHAT TO STUDY?
3. WHO HELPS ME STUDY?
4. HOW DO I STUDY?
5. WHO CAN HELP HOLD ME ACCOUNTABLE TO STUDY?

THE BEST 40 DAYS OF MY LIFE

DAY TWELVE

TEACH

COLOSSIANS 3:16

As a teacher, which we all are based on what we do in our lives as parents, friends, and siblings, we need to understand how valuable it is to learn. Learning is severely undervalued. This ability to learn is taken for granted.

We need to learn from God so that we can teach others. In the previous lesson about study, we know that study is required so that we can be a good steward of what we are designed to do.

Teach with your heart. Teach with compassion. Teach with the sensitivity that you too were once ignorant. Teach with an understanding that if we are educated properly then we do not keep paying for the ignorance of others. Teach through your storm. During your storm is when you are the most sensitive to the needs of others. During the storm is when you are able to share your testimony the best—this is when you are the most authentic.

Our journey teaches others how to start the journey, travel the journey, survive the journey, and share the journey. We teach most often without even saying a word. Our behaviors are on display all of the time, especially when we are not expecting others to notice.

What do you teach others? What do others teach you? What do you want to teach others? What do you want others to teach you?

Jesus teaches us to teach others. Teaching is part of what God calls us to do. We cannot opt out of teaching. Teaching is not optional. If I can help You create a better community, God I am willing to teach others what I know, believe and have experienced. I teach because Jesus taught me.

THE BEST 40 DAYS OF MY LIFE

DEAR GOD,

Thank You for sending Your Son, the Teacher! Lord, You allowed Him to teach me so much. Lord, Jesus teaches me to fast. He teaches me to walk. He teaches me to obey. He teaches me compassion. He teaches me how to avoid temptation. He teaches me how to pray. He teaches me how to love my enemies. He teaches me how to pray. He teaches me how to pray for those who despitefully use me. He teaches me how to walk on water. He teaches me how to weather a storm. He teaches me how to trust.

He teaches me to trust You. He teaches me faith. He teaches me how to manage my anger. He teaches me to forgive. He teaches me how to forgive without limits. He teaches me about You. He teaches me about the Holy Spirit. He teaches me intercession. He teaches me peace. He teaches me love. He teaches me how to serve others. He teaches me to follow. He teaches me to lead. He teaches me to learn. He teaches me how to depend solely on You.

He teaches me how to meditate, retreat, and replenish with Him because He needed to seek You.

He offered us His name when we pray.

Amen.

JOURNAL QUESTIONS:

1. WHY DOES JESUS TEACH?
2. WHY DOES GOD GIFT US TO TEACH?
3. WHAT IS EFFECTIVE TEACHING?
4. DOES TEACHING BRING ME IN CLOSER RELATIONSHIP TO GOD?
5. DOES GOD CARE IF I TEACH?

The Best 40 Days of My Life

DAY THIRTEEN

DISCIPLE

MATTHEW 28:19-20

Pass on to others what I have taught you. If I am paraphrasing correctly, Jesus is sharing that we have been selected as His disciples. Jesus shared so much with His disciples. At that point, Jesus asked that His disciples that share Him with others, in expectation that they will also become a disciple to serve. As a disciple, we are expected to follow His directions and instructions. His teachings are to be followed and His decrees are to be upheld.

Why don't you want to share what Jesus with others? Openly? Willingly? Eagerly? What happens when we don't share Jesus? Other than being disobedient? Could we be too selfish to share Jesus? Or do we regret to share is because we are too silly? Or do we simply not know enough about God's glory that you not overwhelmingly are compelled to share His goodness to others?

When we do share God, we admit and surrender to God's calling. As a called disciple, we must do the work we are assigned. This is not a job, it is a calling—you cannot quit. This is not optional. Understand that when you opt out of your assignment, then you delay someone else's blessings. You may also delay someone else's introduction to Christ. You are a part of a bigger plan so when you do not participate, you cause a ripple effect in the plan.

As a disciple, we should be excited to share the word of God with others, even if we are afraid to speak to strangers. Keep in mind someone spoke to us and introduced us to God. We know how magnificent God is so why would we not want to do the same for others?

We all have a part so we each need to participate at a high level.

THE BEST 40 DAYS OF MY LIFE

DEAR GOD,

Make me a better disciple! Lord, I want to follow You more closely but I can't seem deny myself and take up my cross daily so that I can follow You.

Lord, forgive me for not following You like I should. Lord, I know that I am disobedient and I do not deserve the benefits of being Your child!

God, I am not sure of all that You have planned for me but I do know that it is only what You can trust me with, is only what I can do with Your guidance and the provision You have made for me to accomplish according to Your will. God, I know that I can think up many things but I really only want to think those details that are of Your will and what You want for me. I do not want to be distracted by the outside activities that do not match to Your will.

God, You called me to be a disciple with certain parameters. I have certain responsibilities but what that means is that I have to work. God, I thank You for choosing me to serve others. Please equip me to follow each of Your decrees and commands. Please stabilize my mind and regulate my heart so that serving will be considered the gift from You, God. Please keep me focused on compassionate and sensitive for others so that I can represent You according to Your will and Your plan.

Forgive me in advance for disappointing You—it is not my desire to sin or disappoint You but if I should, I desire Your forgiveness and redirection!

In the powerful name of Jesus.

Amen.

JOURNAL QUESTIONS:

1. AM I A DISCIPLE?
2. HOW DO I KNOW THAT I AM A DISCIPLE?
3. WITH WHICH DISCIPLE DO I MOST IDENTIFY?
4. WHO KNOWS THAT I AM A DISCIPLE?

The Best 40 Days of My Life

DAY FOURTEEN

GIFTS

1 CORINTHIANS 12; 1 CORINTHIANS 14:12

You are gifted! No matter what you were told and what you believe, God gifted you—not anyone else gave you the gifts you have. You did not create them yourself either. God created you with these gifts because God has plans for where you will use these gifts.

If you have no idea that you were gifted, let us understand that you are gifted. Your gifts are designed to serve God through others.

God give gifts for us to use to serve and glorify Him. Our gifts are awesome and specifically designed for our personality. Our gifts drive us to serve others in ways we really enjoy.

If you do not know what your gifts are, then there is a spiritual gift inventory which will share with you what those gifts are. Otherwise, the inventory results will help you to understand how to use your gifts. Each of us is responsible for using our gifts when we are called to serve. You may need training to effectively use those gifts. For example, the gift of preaching and exhortation should seek formal seminary training.

Use your gifts with your whole heart. Give your gifts away freely! They were given to you by God. You will not run out. Do not be stingy! Realize that with gifts, we are on assignment to each other. You want the person designed to bless you to be on time and selfless. You need to do the same.

Your gifts are great investments from God into your life. God trusts you with these gifts to use them for Him, for His plans, in His timing, and to complete His work!

THE BEST 40 DAYS OF MY LIFE

DEAR GOD,

I like gifts! I am a commercial person! Lord, I like Your gifts more! Lord, when I consider how You bless me with gifts, I do not always recognize them as they are given or manifest in my life.

Lord, I know that You are My Source for all that I need or desire. Thank You for giving me gifts to give to others. I have more gifts than the average person. With that being said, I am reminded that You give me gifts to help give others a hope and reuniting those who cross our paths with You, Lord God.

Lord God, thank You for lavishing me with the gifts. Thank You for reminding me that they are from You to advance Your kingdom. Remind me not to be selfish or forgetful about my gifts. Remind me to use and not neglect them. Remind me not to brag, be boastful, or tease others who want my gift. Also God, please remind me not to be arrogant when people complement me about my gifts and how You have blessed me.

Lord, as You bless me to bless others, please keep me humble, remind me to give You all of the honor, glory and praise. Thank You for awesome opportunities to share Your gifts with others.

In Jesus' name.

Amen.

JOURNAL QUESTIONS:

1. AM I USING ALL THE GIFTS GOD HAS GIVEN ME?
2. HOW DOES GOD WANT ME TO USE MY GIFTS?
3. WHAT DO I DO THAT INTERRUPTS THE USE OF MY GIFTS?
4. WHAT PREVENTS ME FROM USING MY GIFTS?
5. IS GOD PLEASED WITH MY SERVICE WITH MY GIFTS?

THE BEST 40 DAYS OF MY LIFE

DAY FIFTEEN

GOD'S VOICE

1 SAMUEL 3; 1 SAMUEL 16:1

This is a BIG question for believers: when will I hear from God? How do I know God is talking to me? Why can't I hear from God?

God's voice is strong and powerful. God is clear and concise. God speaks specifically to you. This is not a group message. When you hear God's voice for the first time, you may be startled.

Recall a time you questioned a voice you heard, then what you heard took place. You need to be able to listen more carefully. The ability to hear God's voice includes you being quiet and being still. Keep in mind that God's voice may seem different for everyone but one aspect is true for everyone: God is not going to talk over your arguing, loud music and nonsense!

Can God talk loudly enough to drown out your own mind's voice? Can God talk loud enough to outweigh those outside voices which sometimes is counterproductive?

God's voice is powerful but sometimes quiet. God may whisper and speak volumes. God may stop events from happening so that you can hear His voice.

Are you ready to hear God's voice? God's voice has directives and comfort; discipline and peace; life and love. God speaks and things happen; situations happen; situations change. God's words are all powerful. Nothing escapes God once He has spoken.

When you request to hear God's voice, prepare to change your life and your direction. When you request to hear God's voice, be ready to be silent and to be still.

God's voice demands work and discipline. Those to whom God speaks, consistently obey Him and honor Him through behavior and attitude.

THE BEST 40 DAYS OF MY LIFE

DEAR GOD,

Your voice is so sweet. Lord, when I first heard You call me, I was afraid. And excited. And overwhelmed. Lord, now when I hear You, I am still afraid, excited and overwhelmed, but now I am also surprised when I hear Your voice. Even though I sin and disappoint You, You still talk to me. You still call upon me to do Your work and serve others. You still find me when I am completely lost and have wandered away from Your guidance and protection and when You find me, You speak to me.

Lord, thank You for talking to and considering me to do Your work. Thank You for making me sensitive enough to hear Your voice.

Lord, I recall when Samuel heard Your voice for the first time. It challenged my life too. Lord, when I explain what You sound like, the word sweet keeps popping up. Your voice is exquisite and profound and powerful and prolific.

Lord, thank You for trusting me to hear You. Thank You for trusting me to do Your work. I am thankful for Your forgiveness. I am grateful for Your plans for my life.

I am listening. I pray to hear You accurately.

In the powerful name of Jesus!

Amen.

JOURNAL QUESTIONS:

1. WHAT DOES GOD SOUND LIKE TO ME?
2. WHAT IS GOD SAYING TO ME THAT I AM TRYING TO IGNORE?
3. WHAT DID I HEAR GOD SAY THAT I AM TRYING TO REVISE AND THAT I HOPE GOD WILL CHANGE?
4. WHAT IS THE COST OF IGNORING GOD'S VOICE?
5. HOW DO I DISCERN GOD'S VOICE OVER THE NOISINESS IN MY HEART AND MY MIND?

The Best 40 Days of My Life

DAY SIXTEEN

LOVE: THE DEMONSTRATION

1 CORINTHIANS 13; 1 PETER 4:8

Love is a verb which requires a demonstration. In order to love, there has to be some actions; some behavior indicating that love is present. Someone who wants love should be prepared to love as well. Where you desire love but are not receiving it as you desire, please consider that you have to be able to love.

If you consider each detail of the definition of love, there are two questions we must answer. How much of this definition am I? How much of this definition do I lack?

Becoming the definition of love which God created requires work—your work! You have to work on being the definition. What does it take to become the complete definition of love? Take it one word at a time. Part of the definition is that love is patient, kind, does not envy, does not boast, and it is not proud. Of those five details, which ones do you possess? Today you may be kind, impatient, but not non-envious, boastful and proud. We need to work on three of the five details. Then you work on them one at a time. The key is who do you know who is patient, not boastful, and non-prideful. Those persons can help you with those areas.

Does love start with you loving yourself? Does love start because God loved you first? The people who you define as loving, how do they do it? Why are you not loving or the definition of love? Can you love if you decide to?

If love is as simple as those details, why are we struggling? If love is effective in solving our real struggle, then why do we lack love? Why are not we more motivated to loved based on what love has the power to accomplish? Ask God to lead You to love, to urge you toward love, and to help you share love selflessly.

The Best 40 Days of My Life

DEAR GOD,

While I am yet a sinner, You demonstrated Your deep love for me by sacrificing Your Son so that my future debt would be paid. And I still disobey. Lord, I am grateful but I did not demonstrate that love.

You said if I love You then I would obey your commands. I say I love You and daily I sin. How do I reconcile my love for You while I sin against You?

Lord, I love You and I need You to continue to demonstrate Your love for me. Lord, help me keep my desire to sin low and my sins to none so that I can demonstrate my love toward You.

Lord, I want to live faultless before You while on this Earth. I pray to love You as You designed me to love You.

Lord, I pray that You forgive me when I do not love like You deserve, yet I ask for your love and love without condition.

Lord, thank You for defining love for me so that I can use that to determine whether people love me or not.

I thank You for Jesus Christ and the Holy Spirit who complete Your love for me. DAILY.

In Jesus' name.

Amen.

JOURNAL QUESTIONS:

1. HOW DO I DEMONSTRATE THE LOVE YOU HAVE GIVEN FOR ME TO GIVE TO OTHERS?
2. HOW DOES GOD DEMONSTRATE HIS LOVE TOWARD ME?
3. HOW DO I ACCEPT GOD'S LOVE?
4. HOW DO I ACCEPT GOD'S LOVE ESPECIALLY WHEN I DO NOT LOVE MYSELF?
5. HOW DO I REACH AN UNDERSTANDING OF 'LOVE EXTRAVAGANTLY'?
6. WHY DO I HAVE A PROBLEM LOVING FREELY?
7. WHY DO ACT LIKE I AM THE AUTHOR AND REPLENISHER OF THE LOVE I AM DESIGNED TO GIVE AWAY?
8. DO I TREAT LOVE AS THE VERB THAT IT IS?

THE BEST 40 DAYS OF MY LIFE

DAY SEVENTEEN

A WALK

MATTHEW 14:22-28

A walk. A walk on water. A walk on water made possible because of faith and God's will. Peter was bold enough to ask the question. Jesus said come. Peter walked out on the water. Peter was almost to Jesus when Peter got distracted and started to drown.

We are all Peters. We ask the bold questions, such as a new job, a spouse, a house, a degree, and a child. We ask God and then start the process but get afraid of the blessing. The hardest part is asking the question.

God invites you daily to come but we ignore Him. We do not recognize Him or His voice when He says come. God wants to bless us in the manner in which we asked but sometimes we forgot we asked.

God will only show you the way. He is not going to do the work as well.

Do you thank God for answering you when you ask the bold questions?

Do you recognize that God answers your boldest of requests?

Do you consider what happens when God answers you and you share what God has done? Do you know that your family, friends, co-workers, and other people near you are watching? Do you know that your response dictates how others will respond to 'God's response'?

Imagine what the other disciples were thinking as Peter was walking on the water. Why didn't I think of that? What is going to happen next? I wonder if I could walk on water too? Why does Peter always have these experiences? In front of us? Why am I scared? What do I need so that I could talk to Jesus like Peter? What do I have to do so that God will say come? What is distracting me from asking/responding to God when I need to be walking on water? How can I remain focused on Jesus so that I do not fall before I reach the finish line of Jesus?

THE BEST 40 DAYS OF MY LIFE

DEAR GOD,

These are some of my favorite verses of scripture where Jesus invites Peter out on the water. Lord, I am reminded that You invite me to walk on water with You daily.

Lord, help me to remember it is You on who I rely and it is you on whom I depend on daily for the walk You have designed and prepared especially for me. Lord, help me remember that You already planned this walk and considered all of the possibilities this walk holds for me.

Lord, thank You for inviting me—trusting me enough to invite me to walk with You. I realize that I do not deserve this invitation. I realize that You know me and all of my thoughts so You know the battle that exists within me to follow You and do Your will and walk accordingly.

Lord, thank You for saving me from falling when I am walking on water with You! Thank You for helping me from my fallen spiritual walk and my fallen mental disposition.

Lord, thank You for holding me accountable for my lack of faith and overall activity. Lord, remind me that I challenge You for some of these invitations so excuse me when I doubt because You oblige my challenge and then it goes better than expected.

Remind me Lord God that this is Your walk!

In Jesus' name.

Amen.

JOURNAL QUESTIONS:

1. WHEN GOD INVITES ME TO 'WALK ON WATER,' WHY DO I DOUBT GOD'S ABILITY TO SUPPORT ME WHILE I WALK?
2. WHEN HAVE I NEGLECTED TO TRUST GOD AND 'WALK'?
3. HAVE I ASKED FOR FORGIVENESS FOR MY SIN OF AVOIDING GOD'S WILL?
4. GOD, WHERE DO YOU WANT ME TO 'WALK'?
5. GOD, WHO DO YOU WANT ME TO 'WALK' WITH?
6. WHAT DID I LEARN ON THE 'WALK'?
7. WHO WILL SEE ME 'WALK' AND BE BLESSED BECAUSE OF MY FAITH?
8. WHO HAVE I WATCHED 'WALK'?

_____
_____
_____
_____
_____
_____
_____
_____
_____
_____

The Best 40 Days of My Life

DAY EIGHTEEN

HEALING

LUKE 8:42B-48

Healing is a magical moment. It is the collision of God's decision and His hand on your life coupled with your surrender! Healing is purposed and intentional, not accidental or incidental. God has plans for your healing. Do you plan to surrender? Today? Right now? Without excuse?

Are we like the women in the scripture? Will we recognize God for the healer that He is?

At the point when she surrenders to Jesus, she had given all that she had to doctors and whatever other methods she could think of. But upon hearing about Jesus, she sought Him with all that she was and with nothing. She was willing to do what was necessary to be healed.

Are you willing to surrender to God for your healing? Are you willing to leave the hurt and pain behind?

Are you willing to seek God to heal you? Is your healing waiting on your surrender?

Do you FULLY believe that God is your complete healer?

Do you understand that God is healing you for His glory, not your comfort and convenience?

Are you willing to share your testimony for His work within you?

Healing is an expression of God's power. Healing depends on your total surrender. Are you able to completely trust God so that He can heal you? What are you going to do when God calls your name? God calls us unto Himself at all times, but we often miss the opportunity to answer God.

Healing requires you to be present. She acknowledged that she was OUT of options. Then she heard about Jesus. She was willing to trust Jesus. She was willing to risk public shame to reach Him. She was willing to get caught seeking Jesus. She was in need of her Healer—she touched the Hem of His garment. When Jesus called for her, she wanted to be overlooked and ignored and forgotten. But because Jesus continued to call for her, she answered. Then Jesus affirmed her physical healing but when Jesus called her daughter, Jesus healed her broken heart and broken spirit.

The Best 40 Days of My Life

FATHER GOD,

I am in need of healing from You! Lord, I have a broken heart which I put in the wrong hands and trusted the wrong source.

Lord, I have a broken mind. Lord, my thoughts are not pure. My mind is not set on You. Lord, I need You to retrieve my mind from the dark places it travels. Lord, bring my mind under subjection to You.

Lord, keep me focused on You in all that I do. I need to keep You on my mind so that I do not stray from Your path—the one prepared and planned specifically for me.

Lord, heal me of my broken spirit. I need Your healing. With so much daily disappointment, and regular disappointment, I need Your healing. With one touch, You make my day bright Lord. With Your touch, Your voice, You make my spirit healthy, whole, and wise. Lord, help me avoid the places and people which cause me to spiritually falter or enter spiritual bankruptcy.

Lord, I want to be physically whole. You said that I would prosper as my soul prospers. Help me heal physically and within my soul.

Lord, I want my soul to cry out to You and seek You authentically because I love You and seek to serve to You!

Lord, I know that You can restore me back to Your settings right now in Jesus' name!

Amen.

JOURNAL QUESTIONS:

1. THANK YOU GOD FOR HEALING ME. WHAT HAVE YOU HEALED ME FROM?
2. WHAT WILL YOU HEAL ME FROM?
3. HOW DO I SUBMIT TO YOUR HEALING BETTER?
4. HOW DO I WAIT ON YOUR HEALING?

The Best 40 Days of My Life

DAY NINETEEN

STILL

PSALM 46:10

"Being still and doing nothing is not the same thing." Karate Kid (2010)

Being still is an art that God equips you to master. The ability to be still is how God knows we are totally dependent on Him. Gage defines being still as not meddling in God's affairs—especially when it concerns you! Being still is not forcing the outcome. Being still is following directions from God. Being still is not rushing the process. God is on His own timing. God's timing cannot be altered by anyone. Interfering is not helpful and is the opposite of being still. If you are not peaceful about what you are doing then you are not being still.

God does not need your help! He can be God without any assistance. No, you cannot do it better than God. You do not know better than God—especially about yourself. You do not know the bigger picture nor the entire plan.

When you start down that road, you are in trouble! God tells us enough for us to be still.

We normally falter when we get anxious or worry about what God is doing or going to do and when is it going to happen. None of this is our business. We need to be focused and concerned with the place we are in at the time.

Be still about the matter and experience God's peace. If you are peaceful about all of your situations, then you are still. Worry is not still. Constantly thinking about it is not still either.

The Best 40 Days of My Life

FATHER GOD,

Oh Lord, My Lord! How excellent is Thy name in all the Earth!

Lord, thank You for the still waters which restore my soul. I needed that! I needed You to restore my soul. I needed You to revive my spirit. That happened because and when I am still.

Lord, thank You for helping me to be still. Lord, thank You for my stillness in the midst of my storms. Thank You for reminding me of the power of Your stillness.

Lord, I am reminded of the benefit of being still. You are the Great I Am. When You see me be still, You honor that stillness with Your desired outcome. When You still me, You bless me with Your voice in my heart, my mind and my soul. That stillness is how You get my attention and how You address my needs. Like a doctor's anesthesia, You put my surroundings on pause so that You can have my full focus and undivided attention.

Thank You for my stillness—voluntary and involuntary. Thank You for those times when I rejected Your stillness and You met me at my point of need. Thank You for what You reveal in our still time. Thank You for the changes You make while I am still. Thank You for Your attention to me and my needs and desires.

Thank You for Jesus as a still example! In His name, I pray.

Amen.

JOURNAL QUESTIONS:

1. WHAT DOES 'STILL' LOOK LIKE?
2. WHAT DOES GOD WANT ME TO DO WHILE I AM 'STILL'?
3. WHAT IS GOD DOING WHILE I AM 'STILL'?
4. HOW LONG DO I HAVE TO BE 'STILL'?
5. WHAT AM I DOING INSTEAD OF BEING 'STILL'?
6. HOW IS THAT WORKING FOR ME?
7. DO I WANT GOD TO 'STILL' ME?

THE BEST 40 DAYS OF MY LIFE

DAY TWENTY

ENEMY

PSALM 23:5; MATTHEW 5:44-45; PROVERBS 24:17; PROVERBS 25:21; 1 TIMOTHY 5:14

God permitted satan to test Job. In this situation, and the similar situation where Jesus told Peter the devil has asked to sift you (Luke 22:31), the enemy had to seek consent to test them. he still does need God's consent.

With the same consideration, will you agree that the enemy had asked to sift you? Do you understand that while we define the enemy differently, we can agree on the enemy as someone who is causing us to question our relationship with God.

Let us not get an enemy confused with a mere distraction. Enemies are usually long-term and requires our prayer and love. Jesus commands that we love them and pray for them. Jesus challenges that we can love anyone but when we love and prayer for our enemies, we have grown spiritually.

God shares that we are to feed our enemies and provide for their thirst. This is also very hard but again demonstrates our obedience and our spiritual maturity.

We walk in faith that the consent that God give for me that God will also omit our souls. We belong to God. God trusts us and wants to help us to trust ourselves. God is training us for the plans He has for us.

Do not cheer when the enemy fails. The Lord created them as well and will certainly correct them when they have sinned.

Just be sure that you are not defined as an enemy. This is when we forget how easy it is to be used by the enemy.

The Best 40 Days of My Life

FATHER GOD,

Forgive me for being an enemy! For causing adversarial relationships with others! For defining persons as enemy before I know their motives and intents.

Lord, make me sensitive to know who my enemies really are. Lord, if it be Your will, show me why they are my enemy. Lord, distinguish for me an enemy and someone who is just not on my side. Lord, as You reveal these persons to me, help me to seek Your face on how to handle them, individually and collectively.

Lord, help me to forgive those who have wronged me. Lord, position my heart and my mind such that I can forgive immediately and without condition.

Lord, I know that they persecuted Jesus so I know that I am not exempt from enemies—as close as family and as far as the unknown. God, as I anticipate enemies, please prepare my heart when my enemy is as close to me as Judas was to Jesus. God, prepare me to seek You in the matters where my enemies seek to undermine me.

Lord, help me to forgive my enemies and to forget their transgressions as You have forgiven and forgotten. Create in my a clean heart oh God, realizing that I am not fighting flesh and blood but against dark world powers and evil forces. When those elements use people, it is not the people that I am fighting but the evil spirit which occupies. I am reminded God that I am fighting but Your Spirit and Might is fighting that battle against those dark powers.

Lastly Lord, help me to love them as You have equipped me to do so. I need to learn to love those who may not love me, who intend to harm me and who mean to discredit me and overall defeat me.

In the ultimate name of Jesus!

Amen.

JOURNAL QUESTIONS:

1. WHY DO I HAVE ENEMIES?
2. WHAT DO I NEED TO DO WITH MY ENEMIES?
3. IS THE ENEMY I NEED TO DEFEAT OR JUST NEED TO TOLERATE?
4. COULD THE ENEMY BE EFFECTIVE WITH FORCING ME TO PERFORM AND BE PRODUCTIVE IN MY OWN LIFE?
5. WHY AM I MAD THAT I HAVE ENEMIES?

THE BEST 40 DAYS OF MY LIFE

DAY TWENTY-ONE

WAR

2 CORINTHIANS 10:3-4

God has defined war differently than we do. While God has been known to equip David to overcome his opponents, God has also equipped us for the spiritual warfare that we encounter hourly. In this spiritual war, God is the target rather than you.

Spiritual warfare is a soul stirring experience when the challenges in your life are designed to stretch you and create change within you.

Keep in mind that you should not take this attack personally. This should be anticipated, expected and received with the intention that God has the plan to share with you how to activate your spiritual weapons.

Spiritual weapons are defined as the Spiritual Armor (Ephesians 6:10-18), prayer, God, Jesus, and the Holy Spirit.

War is designed to cause you to leave God. Events, people and behavior are designed to separate you from God. There are details which are designed to cause us to be drawn away from God.

Can you be lost in a spiritual warfare? The enemy is counting on it. The enemy is counting a number of us walking away from God because of our 'light affliction.' Is your soul for sale? Is your soul negotiable for the enemy? Would you bargain your soul away for social status, acceptance, or anything else?

The war is to be fought under God's guidance, direction, and protection. This war is not personal but there will be some personal learnings from war. Again, this growth is for you but the war is about God.

The war is fought with the Sword—the word of God, God, the Holy Spirit, Jesus, and prayer!

The Best 40 Days of My Life

FATHER,

As You grow and prepare and prune, help me to accurately recognize war, Lord. Lord, keep me calm so I can respond according to Your will and because of Your plan. Lord, I pray my response is a proportionate one considering the weight of the damage I could cause.

Lord, remind me to only engage in wars that You order and orchestrate. Thank You for equipping me to fight in such a way that pleases You.

Father, God, may the outcome of a war bless You and being glory to Your name. May the wars of my children bless You as well. Lord, let me only fight when I am called into battle for the advancement of Your purposes.

God, thank You for preparing me mentally and spiritually for the wars ahead of me.

Thank You for making me a vessel in Your war.

In Jesus' name.

Amen.

JOURNAL QUESTIONS:

1. WHAT DOES WAR LOOK LIKE IN MY LIFE?
2. WHAT DOES GOD EQUIP ME WITH FOR THE WARS IN MY LIFE?
3. WHO AM I AT WAR WITH? WHY THAT PERSON?
4. DID I CHOOSE WAR OR SHOULD I HAVE CHOSEN PEACE?
5. HOW DO I PREPARE FOR WAR?
6. WHEN I DECIDE TO ENGAGE IN WAR WITH OTHERS, DID I GET APPROVAL FROM GOD TO GO TO WAR WITH MY PERCEIVED ENEMY (ENEMIES)?

THE BEST 40 DAYS OF MY LIFE

DAY TWENTY-TWO

ANGER

EPHESIANS 4:26-27

Anger is to be controlled. Anger is an emotion which can be controlled. Anger is an emotion, which can be illogical. Anger is often compulsive and lacks direction, instead spews everywhere.

Anger is the beginning of some errors if you are not in control. Anger is natural. Your actions once you are angry are not natural. Anger creates discontent, malice, mistakes, dissension, hate, anguish and anxiety.

Anger is the opposite of love. Love and anger cannot dwell in the same body, mind and soul.

Anger has the tendency to sin. God wants to avoid these sins. Anger requires energy. This energy could be used to serve God.

Jesus was angry once. Because of these anger, He overturned some tables in the synagogue. Jesus was upset. He showed us how to be angry. Some people have been angry for decades. That energy and time, and lastly, remembering why you are angry is WASTED!

Take action about the anger—immediately: PRAY! Then after you hear from God, you take action. Anger is temporary. Do not sacrifice your health for anger. The real anger would appear when you realize that you thought the anger was mutual. The object of your anger is not angry. While you are angry, they have moved on. You are still in the same place. Decide to live. Move on. Avoid anger.

Decide to love—FORGIVE!

Stop keeping record of wrongs—FORGET!

It does not matter what happened. The sin costs you, not the object of your anger.

THE BEST 40 DAYS OF MY LIFE

DEAR GOD,

Let the words of my mouth and the meditations of my heart be pleasing in Your sight.

Lord, thank You for saving me from the wrath of my anger! Thank You for forgiving me when I am angry. Thank You for helping me address my anger constructively.

Lord, thank You for Your word which keeps me when I have been angry and when I have been angry with the intention to sin.

Lord, help me to forgive others who have angered me both intentionally and accidentally. Lord, allow me to be sensitive to the needs of others such that I am not angered when I should be serving. Lord, I need to be guided with when it is okay to be angry and when my anger will anger You.

Lord, thank You for teaching me to recognize my anger. Lord, thank You for helping me to channel my anger. Thank You for diffusing my anger. Thank You Lord, for helping me to forget my anger.

Lord, thank You for mitigating the damage I have caused when I have sinned due to my anger. Lord, I am working to please You with my words and my heart.

In Jesus' name, I ask these blessings!

Amen.

JOURNAL QUESTIONS:

1. WHAT MAKES ME ANGRY?
2. HOW SHOULD I RESPOND WHEN I AM ANGRY?
3. WHAT DO I DO TO DIFFUSE MY ANGER?
4. HOW CAN I USE MY ANGER TO BE MORE PRODUCTIVE?
5. WHO AM I STILL ANGRY WITH? WHY?
6. WHAT DO I DO TO RESOLVE MY ANGER?
7. WHAT CAN I DO TO NOT BE ANGRY AT PEOPLE AND SITUATIONS?

_____
_____
_____
_____
_____
_____
_____
_____
_____
_____
_____
_____

The Best 40 Days of My Life

DAY TWENTY-THREE

SERVING OTHERS

1 PETER 4:10-11

Sharing was our first lesson taught in kindergarten. Share with people you do not know. Share with people you do not know, with whom you do not have a relationship with, may not even like, but definitely do not know.

Jesus had been on Earth 33 years; picked twelve disciples, whom He did not know, who did not know Him, and shared His Daddy with them. He served them and He loved them. But we avoid and reject the opportunity to do the same.

Why do you hesitate and /or avoid serving others? Is it because no one serves you? That is not your job, gift, or desire? That is an unmerited choice. We are called to serve others! Our service to others is part of the big plan of God's. God gives through people. God is hoping your motives are pure and your entitlements are relinquished.

Your submission to God through others is a love letter to God. Further, when we save others, we partner with God for His will. When we serve others, we do not lose anything. God is our supplier and replenisher of all resources we use to serve others. You may get frustrated and you may be discouraged but God is your strength. Depend on Him. Serving others rewards you in unforeseen ways. Determine how much joy you would like to experience. Joy results from serving others. When you serve others, you learn how to love others.

Serving others also teaches how to be appreciative and grateful. Jesus served others through healing, teaching, washing feet, forgiving us our sins, raising the dead, and Resurrection!

Serving others releases you from your personal bondage.

Serve!

The Best 40 Days of My Life

LORD GOD,

As I serve others, allow me to recall our best example of Jesus Christ, Ruth, Hannah, Samuel, Nathan, Peter and Paul. Lord, these are just a few but Lord, they are our examples of servant leaders. If I am ever at least 25% of who they, I will be pleased with myself.

Lord, I want to serve others with a smile and a heart of gratitude. Lord, I want to share You with others because of my service. I keep those who serve me in my prayers because of my love for You.

Lord, I want to be known as a great servant of You as well as others. Lord, keep me sensitive to You as I serve. Keep me prayerful as I serve others. Lord, keep me humble as I serve others. Lord, keep me focused on You as I serve. Lord, hold me close so that I do not lose sight of why I serve.

Lord, I am certain that I owe You through others. I am eager to serve. Remind of my eagerness when I do not feel like serving or I do not feel like being kind as I serve.

Lord, forgive me for not serving and not being available to Your people when You have assigned me. Lord, forgive me for being too good to serve Your people, especially when I could need that same service.

Lord, I am reminded that Jesus is my example.

In His name!

Amen.

JOURNAL QUESTIONS:

1. WHO AM I SUPPOSED TO SERVE?
2. WHO SERVES ME?
3. WHAT DOES IT TAKE TO SERVE ANOTHER PERSON/GROUP OF PEOPLE?
4. DO I FEEL LIKE I AM GIVING UP PART OF MYSELF WHEN I SERVE OTHERS? WHY?
5. DO I FEEL TOO GOOD TO SERVE OTHERS? WHY?
6. DO I WANT TO SERVE OTHERS? WHY?
7. HOW DO I FEEL WHEN I HAVE GIVEN YOURSELF TO OTHERS?

The Best 40 Days of My Life

DAY TWENTY-FOUR

MINISTRY

MATTHEW 9:37; 1 CORINTHIANS 3:9; COLOSSIANS 3:23

Your ministry is defined as what God has called you to do and how that will be shared with others. Ministry is always in need of helpers, facilitators to move it forward. Ministry is led by people helping other people.

Ministry is work. Hard work. Sometimes without a thank you. Ministry is God's by design. Ministry usually helps others, especially those who cannot help themselves. Ministry is work unto the Lord with all the heart He gives you. Ministry is graded on your attitude toward ministry. Your attitude about ministry is a reflection of how you feel about God. Ministry is a reflection of your relationship with God.

Ministry is an outward exhibit of your appreciation and acknowledgement of God in your life. Ministry is a testimony to others that you believe in God and all that God is is true.

Ministry is designed to grow your spiritual life. This life which will continue to grow closer to God because of Christ is shared when ministry happens.

Ministry is designed to grow your spiritual life. This life which will continue to grow closer to God because Christ is shared when ministry happens.

Ministry is paying back in areas when you benefitted from ministry. Ministry is also paying forward for the blessings that will come your way. We do not expect anything for our service. God does not owe us anything. Ministry will help you reach resolve in any areas of uncertainty.

God equipped and gifted us to serve others through ministry. Ministry is not optional. Ministry often finds you. Ministry answers prayers. Prayers produce ministry.

Ministry requires your intentional heart.

The Best 40 Days of My Life

DEAR GOD,

You have blessed me with a ministry to serve You—not to edify myself. God, thank You for blessing me with a powerful, profound ministry where I share Jesus with others according to Your word and their needs.

Dear Lord, perfect within me the Spirit of discernment when ministry opportunities arise. Help me discern the needs of the people who approach and in front of those I stand. Perfect within me the sensitivity to speak what the Holy Spirit gives to those according to Your will.

Dear Lord, remind me that this ministry I am gifted with is designed to serve You rather than for personal gain. Lord, allow me to understand the mystery of ministry You have given so that I do not get sidetracked or led astray by my own ambitions.

Lord, allow others to see Your light through my words and deeds. Allow others to be drawn to You through the ministry You placed within me. Lord, help me to never disappoint You within this ministry. Lord, usher into me an accountability for others through this ministry.

Lord, I ask respectfully that I am mature enough to respect the gift of Your ministry and all of the 'stuff' that it brings. I want to be responsible with this ministry like Jesus and so many others whom You have blessed.

In Jesus' name.

Amen.

JOURNAL QUESTIONS:

1. WHAT HAS GOD DESIGNATED AS MY MINISTRY?
2. WHAT DOES GOD WANT ME TO DO TO MINISTER TO OTHERS?
3. WHAT DO I DO TO MEET THE NEEDS OF OTHERS?
4. WHAT DO I DO TO MINISTER TO OTHERS?
5. WHO DOES MY MINISTRY HELP?

The Best 40 Days of My Life

DAY TWENTY-FIVE

THE CUP

MATTHEW 26:39

When you consider those areas of struggle in your life, is there anything as powerful or more alarming than Jesus asking to be relieved from 'the cup' which is Jesus' request to not have to die for our sins?

Even if you are dying, you are not going to die for my sins and vice versa. When we are asking to be relieved of anything, even stage four cancer, we need to respect the cup.

The Cup cannot ever be compared to anything else. Jesus was born to die for my sins! Including the sins that I have not committed yet.

When Jesus asked God to be relieved of this cup, I am reminded that I can ask God for anything. My transparency is great for my relationship with God.

David was about to lose his son. He asked God to spare his son. When God answered David, David was able to accept His answer without argument.

Do not continue to despair over small issues or big issues or any issues. Share them with God and leave it there. God is listening. God will hear you. His answer may not be exactly what we want all of the time.

We needed God to say no to Jesus. Sometimes He answers us with a no as well. Because we do not know the future so we do not know the reason why NO is the BEST answer for us at that time.

So when we ask, keep in mind that God has an answer and a reason—which may never be revealed. But if it is revealed, accept God's answer. His big glasses are enough to sustain us from the pain of our cups.

The Best 40 Days of My Life

DEAR GOD,

Your grace is sufficient! Sometimes it does not feel like it, but I know it is.

I pray Your removal of this cup. I thank You for trusting me with Your assignment. I am grateful but I am sometimes unappreciative of that investment within me.

God, when Jesus prayed this prayer to be relieved of the duty of sacrifice, I understood. I understand waiting to give up the cup it not unusual but is not acceptable either.

Lord, I ask that You help me handle my cup responsibly. Lord, help me share the responsibilities of my cup with others so that they can understand Your power and dominion. Lord, as I am used to expand Your kingdom and do Your will, please help me to remain focused on You.

Lord, I thank You for Your grace and Your love. I am grateful for Your investment in me. Your creation of me. Your creation of me overwhelms me. Your giftedness of me overwhelms me and sometimes others as well. You use me profoundly and without my knowledge.

Lord, I love You. While I sometimes do not appreciate my cup and want to be released. I am grateful to serve You and I am careful to give You the praise.

In Jesus' name.

Amern.

JOURNAL QUESTIONS:

1. WHY DID JESUS DO THAT FOR ME?
2. WHAT IS MY CUP?
3. WHAT DOES GOD WANT ME TO DO WITH MY 'CUP'?
4. HOW WILL I SHARE MY CUP WITH OTHERS?
5. WHAT CAN I DO TO OPERATE WITHIN MY LIFE WITH THE 'CUP'?

The Best 40 Days of My Life

DAY TWENTY-SIX

THE FRUIT OF THE SPIRIT

GALATIANS 5:22-23

Of the nine elements of the Fruit, which ones are the easiest for you? Of the elements, which ones are the hardest for you?

All of the elements are required to indwell within each of us. How do we get these elements? How do we maintain those we do possess?

The Fruit makes you easier to get along with and you are a better representative of Christ. It is not easy to operate in all the fruit at the same time. It is possible but I admit difficult.

When we consider the nine elements, which one will you start working on? Have you ever considered your life in these terms? If we are those nine elements, then we are doing what God called us to do.

The hardest elements for me is gentleness and self-control. I am gentle when it is mutual, however when someone handles me roughly then I respond in kind. I will have to learn to trust God more in that area. If you are gentle, what advice do you give to others?

Self-control and the lack thereof is related to all of them. Self-control is important in order to do all of the elements.

We improve with prayer. We remember that God has the big glasses on. God has the power to protect us. The fruit requires surrender to Him—IN All situations! Where we do not surrender to God in order to honor the fruit, we are not trusting God. He can keep us through each situation. The lack of surrender may be why we are in some of these situations we are in.

Fruit requires focus on God. Total surrender will allow the fruit to be evident in our lives.

THE BEST 40 DAYS OF MY LIFE

DEAR GOD,

May You forgive me for sacrificing the fruit of the Spirit for nonsense.

Lord, I have trouble with several elements of the fruit. Father God, I need Your help where I am weak. I need help where I am strong because that strength is where the devil tries to attack.

Lord, allow me to love more comprehensively. Lord, allow me to love when I am hurt and hurting. Lord, keep me focused on why I love—because You love me.

Lord, as I consider my life, help me find the sources of joy. Help me understand the sustainable sources of joy in my life.

Lord, grant me Your peace—Your peace which transcends my complete understanding. Your peace through each and every storm.

Lord, your definition of forbearance, longsuffering. Help me recognize when I need to exercise longsuffering.

Lord, remind me to be kind. Kindness is from You. Allow me to be kind so that others may see You through me.

Lord, help me to be good. My goodness shows You that I am Yours.

Lord, increase my faithfulness! I need Your power with being faithful. I need to show You that I am Yours and believe in Your words and You through my faith.

Lord, help me be sensitive through gentleness and let that gentleness grow so that You are glorified.

Lord, help me exercise self-control. Such self-control is a testimony to You that I am able to be obedient and I respect and love You.

Lord, please hear my prayer.

In Jesus' name.

Amen.

JOURNAL QUESTIONS:

1. DO I EXHIBIT THE FRUIT OF THE SPIRIT?
2. DO I NEED TO DO BETTER WITH A PARTICULAR PART OF THE FRUIT?
3. WHAT DO I NEED TO DO TO BETTER SHARE WITH OTHERS?
4. WHAT IS MY FAVORITE FRUIT OF THE SPIRIT?

The Best 40 Days of My Life

DAY TWENTY-SEVEN

THE ARMOR

EPHESIANS 6:10-18

Armor is designed to protect your body from war. Battle gear. This armor is designed to protect important body parts. God designs His armor differently. God's armor protects all of the body—every part that is essential.

There are six parts of the armor: belt of truth, breastplate of righteousness, readiness of feet from the gospel of peace, shield of faith, helmet of salvation, and the sword of the spirit.

The belt of truth consists of God's truth in the matter. Are you facing God's truth? God's truth is part of the defense against the enemy. We have to know it, recognize it, honor it, and use it. Do not let your version of the truth override the actual truth.

The breastplate of righteousness is God's view of righteousness. The confusion arises when we confuse our version of righteousness with God's. There is no gray in God's definition. God expects us to do the right thing. This righteousness creates a barrier for the enemy because we are not the subject to the guilt which is normally part of the attack.

The ability to move because of the gospel of peace. God's timing when we are moving is remarkable. God keeps us out of harm's way if we remain ready and equipped for movement.

The Shield of faith is difficult to keep in your hand but REQUIRED for the battle where God is protecting you. We normally have the wrong things in our hands when you put the shield down. Doubt and faith cannot exist in the same hands. Keep the shield extended out and up so that you will remain encouraged in the fight.

The helmet goes on your head and is guarded because of salvation. Keep God-centered thoughts in your mind. That helmet guards your thoughts.

The sword of the spirit is the evidence of the battles God has won and the foundation of those He will win. These are the words which bring the enemy under submission. These are the words which offer peace when you are under attack. These are the words which encourage you to show up to battle each day regardless of how bleak the view is.

The Best 40 Days of My Life

DEAR GOD,

Thank You for Your armor, Your protection! Your protection means a lot to me! It is everything to me.

Lord, allow me to be conscious about the enemy while in surroundings and presence.

Lord, remind me that You created the enemy, and You created the protection against the enemy. I need to be faithful to the armor and all of its benefits.

Lord, I want to keep the Sword close to my heart, so that I may know the word by the God I profess to love.

Lord, I often abandon the breastplate of righteousness and the shield of faith because I am busy away from Your will. I need Your hand of protection to remind me about those elements and how necessary they are when I am serving You.

Lord, I want more of an understanding of what You want me to do. Why does the enemy need to attack me? What are You training me for? When will I realize Your plan? And my role in that plan?

Lord, I want to be able to stand against the devil's schemes! I want to fight the way You designed.

For all the battles I have lost because I failed to wear Your armor—Your provision of protection, I pray Your forgiveness.

In Jesus' name.

Amen.

JOURNAL QUESTIONS:

1. WHAT AM I IN NEED OF BEING PROTECTED FROM?
2. WHAT AM I IN WAR ABOUT?
3. WHAT PART OF ME IS A RISK TO THE ENEMY CAUSING THIS ATTENTION?
4. DO I USE ALL OF THE ARMOR?
5. DO I USE IT EFFECTIVELY?
6. WHAT DO I NEED TO BE ARMED AGAINST?

_____
_____
_____
_____
_____
_____
_____
_____
_____
_____
_____
_____

The Best 40 Days of My Life

DAY TWENTY-EIGHT

IMAGE

GENESIS 1:26-27

In His image. In His likeness. You are thinking, 'I am a long way from there.' You may be correct, however, consider what it takes to get closer and how much better you will feel when you are. It takes a decision—your decision—to get closer to God.

First, identify the area(s) which challenge your image the most. Secondly, determine why you are there. Thirdly, ask God to confirm and to reveal those areas. Lastly, ask Him to remove those obstacles and to more closely align us to God. We usually stop at the second step.

One of the reasons that we are still there is because we like it there sometimes and the alternative is Holy. We have a problem with being Holy. It is easier to keep our past and let others do the same. People are waiting for Holy people to fail. Holy people are considered perfect.

There is a huge benefit to pleasing God. There is a huge benefit to honoring God in your image. There is a huge benefit to Holy behavior, mind and soul. The enemy does not attack the same. The enemy does not attack you without God's consent. The hedge of protection does exist and is not simply a prayer cliché.

When you are closer to God's image, your self-esteem will return to healthy. You will be more complete, on your way to whole. The decision to not entertain the enemy will be easier. The desire to entertain the enemy will be less. The mental state and emotional status are elevated and more stable. God's image provides refuge and peace. When you know who to pattern yourself after, there is no confusion and the identity crisis is solved.

God's image is not hard to achieve or maintain. It is the best one to copy.

The Best 40 Days of My Life

DEAR GOD,

Please forgive me for forsaking Your image for what the world defined as great! Lord, thank You for creating me in Your image. Thank you for affirming me through Your image. Lord, I love You for that image and your investment in me.

Lord, forgive me for sacrificing Your image by the clothes I wear that I should not, the words that I utter that I should not and the behavior that I participate in that I should not. Lord, I apologize for embarrassing You based on what I do.

Lord, forgive me for doubting You and Your abilities as Creator—my Creator—and all that You are to me and what You have made me. I am thankful God that You know me. Lord, I thank You for restoring me from all that I have done incorrectly, especially my image.

Lord, remind me that the world does not define me. Lord, help me to avoid the secular trappings that I could easily embody by what I take in through television, music and internet.

Lord, I praise You because I am fearfully and wonderfully made, in Your image, in Your likeness, for Your purpose which You planned in advance.

In Jesus' name.

Amen.

JOURNAL QUESTIONS:

1. DO I MAKE GOD LOOK GOOD?
2. DO I MAINTAIN HIS IMAGE AS I SHOULD?
3. DO I FOCUS ON THE WRONG THING WHEN I CONSIDER MY IMAGE?
4. DO I LOOK LIKE THE PERSON GOD INTENDED?
5. WHAT CAN I DO TO IMPROVE MY IMAGE?

THE BEST 40 DAYS OF MY LIFE

DAY TWENTY-NINE

HIS PROTECTION

ZECHARIAH 4:6; 2 THESSALONIANS 3:3; PSALM 64:1

This cry for protection from the Lord is desperate and emphatic. Mostly because the first person we need protection from is ourselves. Have you ever considered that most of the trouble you are in is the trouble you start? So understand that naturally if the enemy sees that, the enemy considers that a great opportunity to join in.

Then we have signed up for this extra, distraction from the original plan, then we need God. We need God's protection because we got ahead of God and got away from His will. Would we need protection for these issues if we were operating in His will? Probably not.

When God does protect you, will you respond by never returning to the place that required protection? This is important because you recognize that you are not in the right place, that you are being mistreated there, and you are not able to win alone. But when God saves you, deflects the enemy, provides you with relief, what stops you from returning to that same scenario? And if you do, should God save and protect you again?

Protection is on God's terms. At God's discretion. On God's timing. And for God's glory.

We have to lose the mentality that we are so strong and independent. We may impress others but not God. His power is the ultimate one. The might and strength is still a portion, a small portion, of what God has. God's protection should cost us just like it costs us when the enemy has us, but it does not. God accepts us back repeatedly without an issue.

If God's protection is what you need, then you may consider conducting yourself as someone God is proud to protect.

THE BEST 40 DAYS OF MY LIFE

LORD GOD,

I do not know what You protect me from. I have no idea, when I pray that You keep the hedge of protection high around me, all of what that means.

Lord, thank You for protecting me from myself. Lord, I know I cause some of my own pain. Lord, I know that I start my own trouble. Please help me to stop that. I need to stop sabotaging what You have planned for me.

Lord, thank You for the danger that You protect me from that I am aware of—traffic, people, and stuff. Thank You Father when that car goes left, rather than right. And I avoid that accident. Thank You for my leaving home ten minutes later and avoiding that car accident. Thank You for that relationship I said no to which would have led to catastrophic results.

Lord, thank You for protecting me from the danger I will never know and I have never seen. God, I thank You for helping me to understand the comprehensiveness of Your power and dominion. Lord, I thank You for revealing to me that I don't know but a small portion of the complete protection.

Lord, I thank You for protecting me and all that I am.

In Jesus' name, I pray.

Amen.

JOURNAL QUESTIONS:

1. AM I IN A PLACE WHICH COMPROMISES HIS ABILITY TO PROTECT ME?
2. DO I CAUSE MYSELF A NEED TO BE PROTECTED?
3. AM I AWARE OF ALL THAT I NEED TO BE PROTECTED FROM?
4. WHAT DOES HIS POWER MEAN TO ME?
5. DO I RECOGNIZE MY LIMITATIONS?
6. DO I RECOGNIZE GOD'S INFINITE BOUNDS?

THE BEST 40 DAYS OF MY LIFE

DAY THIRTY

HIS PROVISION

JEREMIAH 29:11

God made plans for me. Because God has plans for me, God is also going to insure that those plans will become a reality.

When I look at the evidence of God's plans around me, I am excited and amazed. Because I look at these plans become a reality, I am humbled and submissive.

God created plans for each of us, and while they are not the same, they stem from His love for us.

God provided for Noah and spared his family.

God provided for Hannah and she birthed Samuel.

God provided for David, chose him as king at 12 years old, and blessed him with Solomon.

God provided for Mary and Joseph and gave them a Child, Jesus.

God provided for us when Jesus died and was resurrected in the pardon of our sins—ALL of them.

When God reveals His plan for you, did you reject it because you do not like it or it does not align with your plans? Do you recognize God's plans for you as better for you than your plans?

Do you honor God's plans? Do you ignore God's plans? Do you question God's plans?

Do you submit to God's plans? Willingly? Joyfully? Reluctantly? When opportunities happen which are from God, do you reject them because you did not expect to do that?

How do you realize that God's plans are before you but you are not participating?

Why do you choose differently than God? And expect that path to provide you with what you desire?

God has plans for us—better than we could ever ask or think. What do you risk following God's path versus your own? More or less?

The Best 40 Days of My Life

DEAR GOD,

I thank You for Your unfailing provision in every aspect of my life. Father God, I know that I seem ungrateful most of the time. I forget that You provide for my needs far beyond the measure that I deserve. You continue to provide even when I do not honor You the way I should with what I have.

Lord, I thank You for Your graciousness toward me and Your compassion on me in my situation when I squander Your resources—yet You still give me more.

Lord, help me be the responsible steward over Your resources and I use them as You have instructed and ordained.

Lord, help me to help others when You bless me. I am reminded that You bless those who You can bless through. I want to be a blessing to others as well. Help me to be sensitive to those who need me. Let me be knowledgeable so that I can be available to serve them like others serve me.

Lord, I am reminded that Your ultimate provision is Your ultimate demonstration of love through the sacrifice of Jesus Christ. That provision will last throughout all lifetimes.

Thank You in Jesus' name from my ungrateful self.

Amen.

JOURNAL QUESTIONS:

1. DO I UNDERSTAND WHAT GOD WANTS FOR ME?
2. DO I CONSIDER HOW WHAT I DO INTERFERES WITH GOD'S PLAN FOR ME?
3. DO I GET DISCOURAGED WHEN MY PLANS DO NOT WORK OUT?
4. DO I GET DISCOURAGED WHEN MY FUTURE LOOKS BLEAK WHEN GOD PROMISES GREAT THINGS?
5. DO I UNDERSTAND WHAT GOD WANTS ME TO DO WHILE HE GUIDES ME THROUGH MY LIFE?

The Best 40 Days of My Life

DAY THIRTY-ONE

HIS POWER

EPHESIANS 3:14-21

These are some of my favorite scriptures! When these words penetrated my heart, I wept and surrendered my life to God in an unspeakable way.

His power is at work within me. Paul prays that I be strengthened in my inner being by the Holy Spirit. He continues by praying that I may have power to understand the infinity of God's love. These are some of the most powerful and impactful verses in the whole Bible.

When I consider the power that Paul prays that I have, I am overwhelmed. God is able to empower in my inner being. When I am weak, which is often, I have access to power supplied by God through the Holy Spirit. I need that power in my day to day life. I need to have the help of the Holy Spirit everyday for my life. I am overwhelmed by Paul praying that I will have power to understand how high and long, how deep and wide is the love of Christ. As I try to understand infinity, I really need to understand that I can stop asking does He love me. I can relax that I am loved then I can pursue that which God has planned for me.

With that amount of love, I can do God's will with zeal and fervor. With that amount of love, I can be peaceful. With that amount of love, I can love myself and love myself authentically. With that amount of love and power, I can love others authentically as well. With that amount of love, I can forgive. With all that love, I can accept the love of others. With that definition of love, I can trust the Holy Spirit when He intercedes on my behalf.

With the infinite love understanding, I can stop allowing others to redefine love for me.

THE BEST 40 DAYS OF MY LIFE

DEAR GOD,

As You reveal Your power around me, please forgive me for not respecting it as I should!

Lord, Your power is important to me in every aspect of the word. Help me establish my life such that I experience the fullness of Your power and I share it profoundly and obediently.

Thank You for the power of Your love. You have made infinity so clear to me. Your love and the power of Your love and Your presence. The Power of Your love offers me peace.

Lord, thank You for Paul who pens these verses from Your voice. Just because Paul is able to pen these verses, speaks to Your absolute power. I thank You for the opportunities You let me experience the places where and the times when You exert Your power.

Thank You Father for being the Source of Power we seek for all that we need. Repeatedly. Exponentially. Thank You for being the consistent power in our lives. We know that other powers are inconsistent and incongruent.

Lord, Your power arrests my attention; it subdues my anxiousness and it discombobulates my doubt. Lord, thank You for sharing Your power with me and not withholding it from me.

Thank You for using Your power as You promised when You resurrected Your Son after He was abused by the enemy.

In Jesus' name.

Amen.

JOURNAL QUESTIONS:

1. DO I UNDERSTAND GOD'S POWER?
2. DO I UNDERSTAND GOD'S POWER AT WORK WITHIN ME?
3. DO I UNDERSTAND HOW TO RESPOND TO GOD'S POWER?
4. DO I UNDERSTAND HOW TO ACCESS GOD'S POWER?
5. DO I UNDERSTAND HOW TO EFFECTIVELY USE GOD'S POWER WITHIN ME?
6. IF I DON'T UNDERSTAND THE INFINITY OF GOD'S LOVE, IS MY POWER AND ITS USEFULNESS AT RISK?

THE BEST 40 DAYS OF MY LIFE

DAY THIRTY-TWO

HOLINESS

JOHN 13:10-11; LEVITICUS 11:44

Holiness is an exercise of obedience. Sounds simple? Holiness seems hard to achieve at times. Holiness starts with your view of yourself. We are not holy because we do not view ourselves as available to be holy.

Holiness is defined by God. Jesus furthers the definition. The Holy Spirit confirms the Holiness.

Holiness is the act of being holy. Holy is believing that we can be pleasing to God in our words, deeds, behavior, and emotion. The Holiness we are expected to be is a likeness to God, related to this image. Holy requires effort. It may not always be natural but it is required. Holy is from God for us to embody and embrace.

So how we do move toward holy? Change is required. Where do you start toward holiness?

Music is great place to start. What are you listening to? What are you feeding your soul with? What are you replaying in your mind when you are quiet or in trouble or alone? Is what you are listening to healthy for you? Healthy is defined as uplifting and wholesome. Healthy music does not suggest sin, does not condone sin, and does not prompt sin.

Food is the second place to start. Why is food the resting place and the resort? When used improperly, food can cause all matter of issues from diabetes to high blood pressure, from obesity to low self-esteem.

Relationships are the third place to start. Which relationships are unholy or cause you to respond in an unholy manner? Can you remove yourself from that relationship? If not, can you distance yourself from that relationship? What does it take to get that relationship to healthy?

These are just a small start. We each must examine our lives for the unholy so that we transform and transition to holy—a holy that pleases and represents God.

THE BEST 40 DAYS OF MY LIFE

DEAR GOD,

You are the defining gauge of holiness. I long departed from Your definition before I took any steps, at my first breath.

Lord, honor my feeble attempts to be holy and exercise my limited abilities of holiness. Lord, call me unto You in a mighty way so that I recognize when I am not being holy.

Lord, I want to be holy. In my desire, I get overwhelmed sometimes. Please guide me in Your path to holiness. I need help sometimes understanding that my intentions and my actions do not match. I really need help understanding how to get those two more closely aligned. Lord, I need help with turning away from the unholy behaviors I am tempted to consider.

Lord, show me holiness that pleases You and glorifies You and brings others to You. Lord, help me with holy words and holy thoughts and holy actions.

Lord, keep me focused on how You define holy. Why do I have trouble with holiness? Help me to avoid activities and persons which may influence me to non-holy behavior.

Lord, thank You for giving me an example of holiness in Jesus Christ.

In Jesus' name.

Amen.

JOURNAL QUESTIONS:

1. HOW CAN I BE MORE HOLY?
2. WHAT STOPS ME FROM BEING HOLY?
3. WHAT DOES IT TAKE TO BE HOLY?
4. HOW DOES GOD MEASURE MY HOLINESS?
5. WHAT ARE THE REWARDS FOR MY HOLINESS?
6. WHAT WILL I DO TO BE HOLY?

THE BEST 40 DAYS OF MY LIFE

DAY THIRTY-THREE

FORGIVENESS

LUKE 23:34

The ability, the desire, and the action to forgive is absolute freedom! Keeping track of all those instances and issues is tiring and overwhelming. Keeping track requires time and memory space we could be using for something which honors and glorifies God.

Our lack of forgiveness makes us useless to God. We cannot pray and be heard when we do not forgive. We cannot be forgiven when we do not forgive.

Have you ever considered how much time you have wasted by not forgiving someone? Did you realize that while you are not forgiving them that God already has?

Stop and pray right now for not forgiving others. Call them by name and about which you are holding that grudge. Ask God to help you to forgive them especially because it hurts. Ask God to heal you from that hurt and anguish. Ask God to comfort you when that feeling surfaces again. Ask God to relieve you of those memories which remind you of how you feel.

I want you to consider the fact that when you do not forgive, you are the only one who is hurting. This other person is occupying spaces of your mind, heart and soul and the only person you are punishing is yourself. By not forgiving, you are in bondage! Your decisions are based on this bondage. This is unhealthy and maybe affecting your physical health.

It is definitely affecting your spiritual and emotional health. You cannot give all of yourself to God because portions of you are being occupied by this. You cannot give yourself to others because you measure yourself by what this other person did. All of this is unfortunate.

The person(s) you are not forgiving have moved on and probably do not care. You cannot move on because the best parts of you are in bondage which is preventing God and others from loving and blessing you.

Forgive! You will eat better, sleep better, breathe easier and feel better. You will feel better mostly about yourself.

Forgive!

THE BEST 40 DAYS OF MY LIFE

DEAR GOD,

Please forgive me for the sins I commit against You. Please forgive me for those I commit because I do not know any better—my ignorance.

Lord, I really need the most forgiveness for those sins I continue to commit even when I know I am wrong. Lord, help me overcome the trappings and the temptation over the sin that I find myself so entangled within.

Lord, I am remorseful for those I have hurt, whether intentionally or unintentionally. Lord, help me be sensitive to the needs, hurts and desires of others so that I may respond kindly and Christ-like during their season of need. Lord, for those I have neglected when I promised to assist or serve, please forgive me.

Lord, forgive me of what I do unconsciously regarding worry and fear, doubt and self-pity, worthlessness and low self-worth. Lord, I know these details are not of YOU nor Your word.

Lord, I need to be forgiven for not forgiving others. Lord, help me to release my hostility and anger and grief that I allow to affect my lack of forgiveness of others. I need Your forgiveness so I need to authentically forgive.

Jesus said it and He did it! He can help me too!

In His name.

Amen.

JOURNAL QUESTIONS:

1. DO I ASK GOD FOR FORGIVENESS AS I SHOULD?
2. DO I FORGIVE OTHERS?
3. DO I ASK TO BE FORGIVEN BY OTHERS WHEN I HAVE WRONGED THEM?
4. DO I UNDERSTAND THE CONSEQUENCES OF NOT FORGIVING OTHERS?
5. WHY DO I ALLOW MY LACK OF FORGIVENESS INTERRUPT MY RELATIONSHIP WITH GOD?
6. WHAT STOPS ME FROM FORGIVING OTHERS?

The Best 40 Days of My Life

DAY THIRTY-FOUR

DISCIPLINE

PROVERBS 3:11; PROVERBS 13:24; PROVERBS 15:5; PROVERBS 15:32

For the purpose of our study today, discipline is defined as punishment inflicted by way of correction and training.

If you do not obey, you should expect consequences. Part of the problem is that some of that discipline is immediate and the rest of that discipline is passed to your third and fourth generations. If your questions is, "Is God still doing that?" The answer is because it is in the Bible, I am going to error on the side of yes.

Just consider that you are being punished for something that your great-grandparents did. You may or may not know them. You probably do not know what they did. You cannot escape the wrath of God because of what they did. The thought of that overwhelms me. So with all of that in mind, how can we avoid God's discipline? Secondly, how can we respond properly when we are disciplined?

Let us look at David, our example of God's chosen and beloved. Even David disappointed God because of sin. The first answer is to not sin! When there is a choice—choose not to sin. Easier said than done. I understand.

When God announced David's punishment through Nathan, David's response was, "Yes, Sir." David did not argue or debate. David took an introspective look at himself and his situation, then he submitted to God. David learned that his son would die. David fasted and prayed for seven days, until he sensed the servants were afraid to speak to him. Based on their behavior, David knew that his son had died.

David did not curse God nor did he hold God accountable through questioning for the punishment of his sin. When God kept His word, David simply said okay. David bathed, comforted Bathsheba, and to them was given Solomon. Even after God disciplined David and Bathsheba, God still blessed them.

Accept God's discipline. He still loves you in spite of your sin.

The Best 40 Days of My Life

DEAR LORD,

Please allow me to be the disciple that You desire and You deserve. When I am not the best disciple, I expect Your discipline. Although I do not like it, I do understand that you discipline me because You love me.

God, I know that I disobey regularly, so I receive discipline regularly. I am apologetic that I cannot exercise more self-control in my life and under the influence of others.

God, help me respond to Your discipline graciously and openly. Lord, help me realize that Your discipline is designed to mature me and grow me up in areas where I am lacking wisdom and knowledge.

Lord, remind me that my discipline is also part of my testimony. I will be able to share those with others as part of why I had this experience.

Father God, I bless You for Your love for me. I really need Your love and I do need Your guidance. While I have been out of Your will before, I really need Your help staying in the boundaries of Your will.

Lord God, thank You for loving me.

In Jesus' name, I pray.

Amen.

JOURNAL QUESTIONS:

1. DO I RESPOND OR REJECT DISCIPLINE? WHY?
2. DO I RECOGNIZE DISCIPLINE WHEN IT IS PRESENT?
3. WHOSE DISCIPLINE DO I RESPOND BEST TO?
4. WHY DO I DISLIKE DISCIPLINE?
5. WHY DON'T I SEE DISCIPLINE AS PROFITABLE?
6. HOW DO I USE DISCIPLINE TO GROW?

THE BEST 40 DAYS OF MY LIFE

DAY THIRTY-FIVE

COMPASSION

JOHN 11:35; EPHESIANS 4:32

My daughter is amazingly compassionate. She witnessed a lady get her foot caught in a bicycle. I stepped outside because she had not returned from the car. When I get outside, she is about to cry. I send her back inside to eat but I have to stay with the lady. I cannot return to the dinner table until I have a positive report about the lady and her foot. We try everything, then I get still. At that moment I get still, the Holy Spirit says go get the crowbar. I get the crowbar and wedge it between the pedal and the chain housing, and I pull. I announce that you should be able to move your foot now. She did!

Our job as Christians involves everyone in our paths. If God places someone in your path, it is your now your business. God does place us in questionable situations because it is an exercise of our faith. "Will you trust me that I am Your provider and protector even when your conditions look unsafe and bleak?"

Recalling a time to be compassionate may be hard so I will just share how you can be more compassionate. Let your window down and give the person on the corner the change in your cupholder or a bottle of water or the food you just purchased from Chick-Fil-A, even though you are hungry and you may not have anymore money or you will be late if you go back to the restaurant, or give all of the aforementioned to the person at the corner.

You may be thinking that I am crazy however, we are giving and being compassionate because of God. Your compassion for others is a test of your selflessness and your faith.

You ask God for everything but cannot give away anything? You are only blessed when you are a blessing to others. Hold your hand open. You cannot receive anything when it is closed.

Remember God blesses through people. Be the blessing God allows you to be.

THE BEST 40 DAYS OF MY LIFE

DEAR GOD:

I thank You for Your compassion for me! Lord, I know that may sound selfish, however I am conscious of Your compassion specifically for me. I need Your compassion. I really need Your compassion for my daily life and walk, I am just a breath away from being a deviant. God, I need Your hand of protection around me.

Father God, help me be more compassionate to others who You have placed in my path. Lord, I know how I feel when someone is compassionate to me so I want to be compassionate to others in a likewise manner.

Lord, thank You for Jesus as the Leader of Compassion—Jesus wept. Jesus wept at the death of Lazarus even though Jesus was going to resurrect him. That is the epitome of compassion. I want to be able to have that level of compassion for others because I want that same level of compassion toward me.

Lord, help me be compassionate toward others with such an awesome sensitivity so that I can demonstrate the love that is associated with compassion.

Jesus, thank You for Your compassion. Thank You for Your love toward me.

In Jesus' name, I pray.

Amen.

JOURNAL QUESTIONS:

1. HOW DO I EXHIBIT MY COMPASSION FOR OTHERS?
2. DO I HAVE A PROBLEM WITH OTHERS SEEING ME CRY? WHY OR WHY NOT?
3. DO OTHERS KNOW BEYOND A SHADOW OF DOUBT THAT I CARE ABOUT THEM?
4. DO I EXHIBIT AN UNDERSTANDING THAT MY COMPASSION AND MY LOVE ARE RELATIONAL? DOES MY BEHAVIOR SHOW THIS RELATION?
5. AM I A GOOD EXAMPLE OF COMPASSION?
6. DO MY TEARS STIR THE HEARTS OF OTHERS?

THE BEST 40 DAYS OF MY LIFE

DAY THIRTY-SIX

VICTORY

PHILIPPIANS 4:13-14

People define victory differently because of the circumstances of the victory.

Victory can be sweet if we handle it well. Victory is authored by God. God determines all of the elements of victory. This victory is designed for God's glory. Not for your personal gain. This is hard to digest. We think that victory is for us.

If we are not careful, we will misuse victory. If we are victorious and immature, our mouth may override our position. We need to understand the best way to respond to victory.

Responding to victory requires humility. Humbleness is the best way to respond to victory. Victory does warrant celebration, however it does not warrant bragging or boasting or arrogance. Victory requires God. God gives us strength to do all things that is within God's will.

Victory is going to happen for each of us based on God's will. Victory does not have to be large or outlandish. Further, victory will be realized when God is satisfied with our attitude and work ethic. Victory is not granted when God is concerned about how we will not handle victory well. Victory has to be all-inclusive.

I have a healthy prayer life. I have a healthy study life. I have a healthy meditative life. When I consider these elements, they are good enough to get God's attention. God needs to insure that my motives are pure. Victory shows up in those places.

Victory is not for the selfish, non-Christ-centered and self-motivated.

THE BEST 40 DAYS OF MY LIFE

DEAR LORD,

I thank You for victories both big and small. Lord, I feel so defeated sometimes. You know just the right time to insert a victory so that I can remain focused on You and stay encouraged for service to You.

Lord, keep me encouraged even through my storm. Lord, keep me encouraged when I feel like quitting. Lord, I ask Your covering over me when I am discouraged. Lord, thank You for my growth during these low times. Lord, thank You for the energy to still serve You during these times.

Lord, allow me to remain focused on You as You prepare me and prepare me for my victories. Lord, remind me to be still so that You can work.

Lord, thank You for victories both big and small. I need to remain focused during victorious times! Lord, I thank You for victorious times. I thank You for being able to give You the honor, glory and praise.

Lord, help me remain humble when I am victorious. Remind me that victories are for Your glory as well. Victories are for me to share with others to enhance, renew or stimulate their faith. Victories are not for my personal gain.

Thank You for the victory of Jesus Christ. His victory became my salvation.

In Jesus' name.

Amen.

JOURNAL QUESTIONS:

1. DO I UNDERSTAND THAT VICTORY IS DEFINED BY GOD RATHER THAN BY ME?
2. WHAT I HAVE LABELED VICTORY INCORRECTLY PREVIOUSLY?
3. WHAT WILL I LABEL VICTORY IN THE FUTURE?
4. DOES VICTORY MOTIVATE ME TO MOVE FORWARD WITH MY LIFE WHEN I WOULD OTHERWISE BE DISCOURAGED?
5. DOES MY QUEST FOR VICTORY PUT OTHERS IN JEOPARDY? DO I NEGLECT THEM IN AN EFFORT FOR VICTORY?

THE BEST 40 DAYS OF MY LIFE

DAY THIRTY-SEVEN

REVIVE

PSALM 19:7; ISAIAH 57:15

Revive is defined as to activate to life or consciousness. Revive could mean bring to life. This revival is designed to create life within you that has died because of circumstances and situations.

Do you want your life, your soul to be revived? As we consider the revival of your soul and your life, what was the reason for the death of your spirit and your life?

Do you know that you need to be revived? This is determined by the measure of joy, love, forgiveness, giving, and several other factors. If you are lacking in these areas, we need to understand that our soul needs to be revived.

When we revive a contrite heart, contrite is sincere. When we revive a sincere heart, this revival will be easy to complete. This revival would bring you to life again when you have become less than joyful. When your soul is dead, you cannot praise or worship God. What you give God, while in need of revival, is marginal and limited, unacceptable. When we cannot have authentic worship and praise, then we are limiting God in our lives.

Revive your spirit by reading God's word. Study is next most important. Prayer continually is key to revive your soul. Meditation will allow your heart penetrated.

Revival is important. Keep focused on the healthy soul that God created you with.

Revive!

THE BEST 40 DAYS OF MY LIFE

LORD,

You said in Your word that You would revive the spirit of the lowly and revive the heart of the contrite.

Lord, I am lowly and contrite. Lord, I need reviving! I need You hand of revival right now. Lord God, my Redeemer, I need Your reviving in my life and my heart.

Lord, I need to be revived. I am broken from the last heart break. I am bitter from the family drama. I am bothered from the broken promises those closest to me have uttered. I am bereaved from the deaths of those close to me and those things I have lost. I am broken from the missed dreams and the missed opportunities.

I need a revival from my spirit. My spirit has suffered damage; some of which seems irreparable. My spirit needs You desperately.

I need a revival for my heart. My heart is broken and repair looks bleak. Only You can revive and repair what is damaged and replace what is missing.

In Jesus' name.

Amen.

A Journey of Spiritual Renewal

JOURNAL QUESTIONS:

1. HOW CAN GOD REVIVE ME WHEN I FEEL SO DEAD INSIDE?
2. HOW CAN GOD REVIVE ME WHEN I DO NOT FEEL GOOD ABOUT MYSELF?
3. GOD, PLEASE REVIVE AND REFRESH ME IN THE _____ AREA OF MY LIFE AND WITH THE FOLLOWING PEOPLE IN MY LIFE: _____ _____.
4. GOD, PLEASE REVIVE MY SPIRIT AND SOUL FOR SERVICE TO YOU. WILL YOU PLEASE REVIVE MY SPIRIT AND SOUL?

The Best 40 Days of My Life

DAY THIRTY-EIGHT

HEART

PHILIPPIANS 4:7; PSALM 119:11; PSALM 19:14

Your heart is very important part of your person. Your heart makes decisions that are not subject to change without critical circumstances occurring.

When your heart makes a decision, that is a guarantee. Why does the heart commit at that level? The intensity is profound.

The heart and the mind can disagree from time to time. The heart has to be convinced to change. Sometimes the most logical decisions are ignored because the heart has so much power. When your heart has committed to God, nothing can change your focus. True commitment involves your total heart. God guards our hearts from the areas of our lives which could harm us. God guards our hearts from the things we have committed to that are not good for us.

Our heart needs to please God. The commitment we make needs to represent God's best interest.

Our hearts are not always pure but even if it is not, our hearts are still remarkable. This heart is not an object you can put your hands on. This heart is not a tangible element.

What do you give your heart to? Does that please God? Does it cause you to sin? Does it cause you to seek God fervently? Does your heart offer itself to elements which would distract you from God?

When I say those scriptures, I have to stop and adjust my heart toward God, regardless of how I really want something else. My heart belongs to God. God created me and my emotional being.

God deserves my heart and the best of me!

THE BEST 40 DAYS OF MY LIFE

DEAR GOD,

I thank You for my heart with all of its details, its compassion, its hurts, its pains, its strength, its power, its presence, its magnetism, its proof of life and its energy to serve You.

Lord, forgive me for the unwholesomeness of my heart! I know that it is not pure and I am trying to be more righteous. Lord, please help me to correct my mediocre meditative measures of my heart. I want my heart to please You but Lord, I often fall short.

Lord, You have empowered my heart to serve You through others. Help me to remain focused and committed to Your calling and Your will.

Lord, I live to serve and please You even when my heart is breaking! Everyday, under ALL circumstances, I want my heart healed. I know that I cannot heal myself nor can I help myself out of these pockets of difficulty.

Lord, thank YOU for the love You have embedded in my heart! I can love others in spite of what they do to me and against others.

Lord, help restore me to You and Your Covenant, Master. Master, I need You to insure that I am serving You with my whole heart. Return those parts that have disappeared.

In Jesus' name, I pray.

Amen.

JOURNAL QUESTIONS:

1. GOD, CAN YOU CREATE IN ME A CLEAN HEART, OH GOD, MY ROCK AND MY REDEEMER?
2. WHAT KEEPS MY HEART FROM YOU?
3. WHO OCCUPIES THE SPACE IN MY HEART THAT YOU SHOULD OCCUPY?
4. GOD, CAN YOU HEAL MY BROKEN HEART?
5. GOD, CAN YOU SHOW ME HOW TO MANAGE WHO I LET IN MY HEART?

THE BEST 40 DAYS OF MY LIFE

DAY THIRTY-NINE

WISDOM

JAMES 1:5; I KINGS 3:12; PROVERBS 3:7

Wisdom takes a long time to appreciate. Wisdom is given as requested. Wisdom is given because we can be trusted to use that wisdom, rather the previous method which we make decisions and draw conclusions.

Wisdom challenges old logic. Wisdom creates more positive relationships. Wisdom shares wisdom. Wisdom is giving, caring, and compassionate. Wisdom challenges wrong. Wisdom seeks the God-centered solution. Wisdom is silent at the appropriate time, and speaks at the appropriate time. Wisdom knows when to take a stand and when to be still and wait on God.

Wisdom is graded by our words, deeds, thoughts, and actions. God is the Grader and Giver of our wisdom. We are designed to use it first for God. If it is available to others, then fine. Our wisdom is designed to bring God glory.

Wisdom should preclude us from making mistakes we have previously made and issues we have previously had. Wisdom is dependent upon our submission to using our previous experiences and leadership from God.

Wisdom demands that we do not exercise the same behavior, hang out with the same people, do the same things, think the same thoughts, and pursue the same goals.

Wisdom is designed for us to overcome our idiosyncrasies. Wisdom improves our communication and our love for others. Wisdom answers questions and it solves problems. Wisdom keeps you focused on the main objective and eliminates the ability to get side-tracked and off course.

Wisdom is the investment God makes within us for His use. Wisdom represents Him.

The Best 40 Days of My Life

MASTER,

You have made many promises to me regarding wisdom. You said that if I ask for wisdom that You would grant it to me. Lord, I am asking faithfully, believing that I will be more wise. I offer that I now realize that in order to become more wise, I will have to experience more situations and circumstances where wisdom is birthed.

Lord, remind me that I have to be present to receive Your wisdom. Wisdom requires active engagement. You require my attention—full and undivided.

Your wisdom, God, is worth the walk and the work and the weight of the responsibility. Lord, remind me that Your wisdom has responsibility. Your wisdom does not come to me without the need for me to work.

Lord God, I wish to use my wisdom according to Your will. Your will and wisdom are a couple. One does not work without the other.

Lord, I consider wisdom a gift which everyone is not offered, even some who are offered do not accept, still others are offered, they accept, but they misuse Your gift of wisdom. So I want to be one who recognizes wisdom as a gift, uses it appropriately, and according to Your will.

In Jesus' name.

Amen.

JOURNAL QUESTIONS:

1. GOD, CAN YOU SHARE ME THE PERSONS AROUND ME WHO ARE WISE AND WHO ARE WILLING TO HELP ME TO BECOME WISER?
2. GOD, CAN YOU HELP ME WITH MANAGING MY WISDOM?
3. GOD, MAY I HAVE MORE WISDOM?
4. GOD, HOW DO YOU MEASURE MY WISDOM?
5. GOD, HOW DO OTHERS VIEW MY WISDOM?

THE BEST 40 DAYS OF MY LIFE

DAY FORTY

RENEWAL

2 CORINTHIANS 4:16; ROMANS 12:2

Renewing your mind means that we have to admit there is something wrong and is in need of an adjustment.

What is on your mind? What are you thinking about? Is your first mind related to what we believe Christ would be pleased with?

How do you return to the factory settings? God created you with a pure mind and a pure heart. Little by little, we have distanced ourselves from the place where God originally designed for us.

What happened exactly when You started doubting God? What exactly took place when you decided that you would listen to others and God was just another opinion?

Renewing our minds means that God is priority. God becomes first on your mind. You seek God first when crisis occurs. God comes before the "go-to's." God is the source we seek for the voice we heed when life is going awry.

What does it take for you to return to God? Can you just put your pride and ego aside to return to God? What does it take to return to God so that He can answer your prayers, questions, and needs?

God wants your mind. God wants your mind back. What is it going to take to surrender the asset that directs your whole body to God so that God can do His will?

Your mind is where you store everything—all memories, all excitement, all evidence, all grudge-holding, all disappointments, all dreams, all goals, everything.

Leave the world out of your decision making. The world will mislead you. The world will deceive you.

Return to God!

Renewal is required for a great, whole relationship with God.

THE BEST 40 DAYS OF MY LIFE

DEAR MASTER,

Your renewal means the most to me. In a world which is driven by quick fixes and solutions in a bottle, Lord, I need Your touch. Your hand. Your refreshing and replenishing touch around me so I can be renewed within You.

Lord, I regard renewal highly for this time in my life and in my journey as a Christian. Lord, this world is after my mind and my soul. Lord, help me keep my mind focused on You.

Lord, I regret the things that I take in that is not from You, not of You and not worthy of You. I know that You need me to be focused on You with my mind. You are the Creator of my mind. You have tried to retrieve it through the sacrifice of Your Son then You keep having to ask me for it back—my apologies.

Help my mind think according to Your will. Please help me keep my mind on You and only Your will. Please help me understand Your will can be done through me if I remember to depend on You for all that I need.

Lord, keep me mentally sharp so that I may perform in the world where You have called me to serve.

Lord, keep me mentally sharp so that I can be aware of the devil's schemes.

Lord, I thank You for my state of mind! Renew my spirit to better serve You, Lord Almighty!

In Jesus' name, I pray.

Amen.

JOURNAL QUESTIONS:

1. GOD, WHAT DO I HAVE TO ELIMINATE FOR YOU TO RENEW MY MIND?
2. GOD, WHAT DOES IT TAKE TO REMAIN IN MY RIGHT MIND?
3. GOD, WHAT DOES IT TAKE FOR MY HEART AND MIND TO BE CLEAR?
4. GOD, WHAT DOES IT TAKE TO KEEP MY MIND ON YOUR MATTERS?
5. WHAT DO I HAVE TO CHANGE IN ORDER TO RELINQUISH MY MIND TO YOU?

_____
_____
_____
_____
_____
_____
_____
_____
_____
_____
_____
_____

The Best 40 Days of My Life

REFLECTIONS

1. WHAT SACRIFICES DID YOU MAKE TO COMPLETE THIS 40 DAYS?
2. HOW MUCH CLOSER ARE YOU TO GOD?
3. WHAT WAS THE MOST PROFOUND THING THAT GOD SAID TO YOU IN THIS 40 DAYS?
4. WHAT CHANGES HAVE OCCURRED DURING THESE 40 DAYS?
5. WHAT WILL YOU SHARE WITH OTHERS ABOUT THESE 40 DAYS?
6. WHAT WILL YOU DO TO FOLLOW GOD'S WILL FOR YOUR LIFE?
7. DOCUMENT HOW YOU FEEL AFTER THIS STUDY.

_____
_____
_____
_____
_____
_____
_____
_____
_____
_____

THE BEST 40 DAYS OF MY LIFE

A Journey of Spiritual Renewal

PRAYER REQUESTS ♦ PRAYER JOURNAL

1. WHAT ARE YOU ASKING GOD FOR?
2. WHAT ARE YOU HOPING GOD WILL DO?
3. WHAT ARE YOU EXPECTING FROM GOD?
4. WHAT HAS GOD ALREADY DONE TO EXCEED YOUR EXPECTATIONS?
5. WHAT HAS GOD DONE TO GET YOUR ATTENTION?
6. WHAT HAS HE SHOWN ABOUT HIMSELF AND YOU?

The Best 40 Days of My Life

A Journey of Spiritual Renewal

The Best 40 Days of My Life

A JOURNEY OF SPIRITUAL RENEWAL

THE BEST 40 DAYS OF MY LIFE

INDEX

Reference	Page	Reference	Page
2 Chronicles 7:14	41	Leviticus 11:44	149
Colossians 3:16	69	Luke 8:42b-48	93
Colossians 3:23	117	Luke 23:34	153
1 Corinthians 2:9	37	Matthew 1	29
1 Corinthians 3:9	117	Matthew 5:44-45	101
1 Corinthians 12	77	Matthew 6:16-18	45
1 Corinthians 13	85	Matthew 9:37	117
1 Corinthians 14:12	77	Matthew 14:22-28	89
1 Corinthians 14:26-40	57	Matthew 14:31	49
2 Corinthians 4:16	181	Matthew 26:39	121
2 Corinthians 10:3-4	105	Matthew 28:19-20	73
Ephesians 3:14-21	145	1 Peter 4:8	85
Ephesians 4:26-27	109	1 Peter 4:10-11	113
Ephesians 4:32	161	Philippians 4:7	173
Ephesians 5:25-27	37	Philippians 4:13-14	165
Ephesians 6:10-20	129	Proverbs 3:7	177
Galatians 5:22-23	125	Proverbs 3:11	157
Genesis 1	25	Proverbs 13:24	157
Genesis 1:26-27	133	Proverbs 15:5	157
Hebrews 11:6	49	Proverbs 15:32	157
Isaiah 57:15	169	Proverbs 24:17	101
James 1:5	177	Proverbs 25:21	101
Jeremiah 29:11	141	Psalm 1:1-2	61
John 1:1-2	29	Psalm 19:7	169
John 3:16	37	Psalm 19:14	61
John 11:35	161	Psalm 23:5	101
John 13:10-11	149	Psalm 46:10	97
John 16:5-16	33	Psalm 95:6-7	57
1 Kings 3:12	177	Psalm 100	57

THE BEST 40 DAYS OF MY LIFE

Psalm 117	53
Psalm 119:11	173
Psalm 139:14	53
Romans 12:2	181
1 Samuel 3	81
1 Samuel 16:1	81
2 Samuel 12:21-23	45
1 Timothy 5:14	101
2 Timothy 2:15	65
Zechariah 4:6	137

RESOURCES

www.biblegateway.com

www.onediagage.com

THE BEST 40 DAYS OF MY LIFE

ACKNOWLEDGEMENTS

God, thank You for Your plans for me. Thank You for **The Best 40 Days of My Life** and choosing me to complete Your project. I just want to please You. Thank You for continuing to anoint me and to invest in me and my gifts, which keep surprising me. Thank You for loving and forgiving me.

Hillary and Nehemiah, thank you for supporting me and my endeavors. Thank you for loving me, especially when I do nothing without a pen and a clipboard, thank you for enduring my late nights, your ideas, the sounding board, the love and the support. Thank you for celebrating our legacy.

To my prayer partners and to my accountability partners, thank you for the long talks and the powerful prayers and the encouragement. To my pastor and church family, thank you so much for your love and support.

The Best 40 Days of My Life

Minister Onedia N. Gage seeks to share her outlandish pursuit of God with her prayers, study and meditation. She desires to share her faith in a manner which helps you do the same through her calling. She hopes that these words bless you.

Please feel free to contact and share your testimony. onediagage@onediagage.com, or @onediagage (twitter). www.onediagage.com

Blogtalkradio.com/onediagage

Youtube.com/onediagage

Facebook.com/onedia-gage-ministries

THE BEST 40 DAYS OF MY LIFE

A Journey of Spiritual Renewal

Preacher ♦ Prayer Warrior ♦ Teacher

Small Group Leader

To invite Rev. Gage to preach, teach, and pray, Please contact us at

@onediangage (twitter) ♦ onediagage@onediagage.com ♦ facebook.com/onediagage

youtube.com/onediagage ♦ blogtalkradio.com/onediagage ♦ www.onediagage.com

The Best 40 Days of My Life

Publishing

Do you have a book you want to write, but do not know what to do?

Do you have a book you need to publish but do not know how to start?

Would publishing move your career forward?

Let us help

onediagage@purpleink.net ♦ www.purpleink.net

512.715.4243

www.ingramcontent.com/pod-product-compliance
Lightning Source LLC
Chambersburg PA
CBHW080450170426
43196CB00016B/2741